"I encourage all coaches and managers to read this ... Alexander, Founder of Business Coaching in Eu ... GROW Model

"This is a 'must read' for any coach who is serious about achieving hard core business results." - Kay Cannon, MBA, ICF Master Certified Coach & 2007 Global President, International Coach Federation

"This book is a refreshing, provocative approach that challenges the coach, as well as the coachee, to be accountable for results." - John Leary-Joyce , CEO, Executive Coach & Supervisor, Academy of Executive Coaching

"This is a truly excellent book for the experienced leader and coach." - Jonathan Perks, MBE, Managing Director Board & Executive Coaching, Penna plc

"Reading this clear and pragmatic book has helped me chart my way through the troubled waters we find ourselves in." - David Megginson, Professor Emeritus, Sheffield Hallam University's Coaching and Mentoring Research Unit

"Coaching comes of age!" - Liz Macann, 'Coaching at Work' coach person of the year, 2008

"Any coach who truly wishes to serve their client and succeed in the corporate world cannot afford to ignore the messages contained in this book." - Jackie Barnacle, Internal Coach & Change Programmes Director, Logica plc

"This book will be an important item in the toolkit of any coach training towards accreditation." - Mike Hurley, Director, Intuition Discovery and Development Ltd & President, European Mentoring & Coaching Council, UK

"This book expands established coaching skills to focus on 'bottom-line' results whilst contributing to the continuous evolution of the coaching profession." - Carsten Ohrmann, Global Account Director, Logica plc and Chairman of CxO-Coaching

"This book is a reminder of the need for coaches, and our evolving profession, to continually evaluate what we do, to 'hold the bar high' and to be conscious of the broader context." - Katherine Tulpa, Founding Chair and CEO, Association for Coaching & Co-Founder, Wisdom8

"If you're expecting a fluffy 'how to be a better coach' guide, forget it. A true wake-up call for the coaching profession." - Verity Gough, Editor, TrainingZone.co.uk

Where were all the coaches when the banks went down?

Advanced Skills
for
High Performance
Coaching

John Blakey & Ian Day

Edited by Alice Hurley

Foreword by Sir John Whitmore

Where Were All the Coaches When the Banks Went Down?

By John Blakey and Ian Day

Edited by Alice Hurley

For more information visit www.121partners.com

ISBN: 978-1-4452-1597-6

Copyright © 2009 121 Partners Limited

Contents

Foreword

This is not another book with a new angle on the banking crisis, but one that uses the issue to question the role and responsibility of coaches generally. The title suggests that coaches might have been more courageous and done more to warn about, help or even avert the problem. The book aims to upgrade the skills, and thereby the confidence, of existing coaches. To do this it assumes the reader is familiar with the basics and principles of coaching and enters the fray a level higher, addressing more complex or controversial issues.

In defence of coaches, we can also reverse the title question and ask why the bankers did not seek more coaching, or any other advice come to that? I myself, wrote a well circulated article on the coming economic crisis in 2005 entitled 'Denial and Demise' but no bankers read it! It is precisely because the bankers were so poorly informed and such 'silo' thinkers that they failed us all so badly. Let us hope that bankers use more coaches in future. This book tells coaches what they could be doing - and how - for all too often we shrink from challenging our clients when in fact a challenge would be both appreciated and beneficial.

Importantly it challenges coaches too by giving them permission to break a 'golden rule' of coaching, that of staying on the coachee's agenda exclusively. It actually encourages breaking it. I wholeheartedly agree with this. A coach's task and responsibility is not only to benefit the coachee, but also the client company and all of society too - hence the title.

This is a brief, well written guidebook to executive coaching that can be digested in a couple of hours, which is 'a breath of fresh air' in these times when there is never enough time. John and Ian give guidance about the more sophisticated aspects of coaching, and about the kind of questions good coaches can usefully ask, providing illustrative examples. The FACTS in the book are clear and this useful model is well laid out and easy to grasp. Hopefully, it will be a roadmap for coaches to use to venture into the less charted territories of conventional executive coaching.

This philosophical and professional approach to coaching is to be admired. I am glad that others will now have the opportunity to gain from Ian and John's experience and expertise through this very readable account. Read on....

Sir John Whitmore

Author of 'Coaching for Performance', Chairman of Performance Consultants International

Acknowledgements

We would like to thank our colleagues in 121partners for helping us shape our ideas and supporting us through this process. In particular, we would like to thank Alice Hurley for her contribution in editing the book with great attention to detail and discipline. We would also like to thank our clients for providing us with the experience and feedback which led to the development of the FACTS approach. Last but not least, we would like to thank our families for the inspiration and love that enabled this book to happen.

Ian & John

About This Book

This book is primarily for experienced executive coaches and buyers of executive coaching who are supporting senior leaders in large, complex organisations. It is also aimed at those business leaders who have embraced a coaching style and wish to continue to evolve their skills to meet the demands of the new economic environment.

The book assumes a knowledge and experience of basic coaching skills and models. For example, readers will already be familiar with common coaching models, such as GROW, and will have attended 'Introduction to Coaching' style courses. It also assumes that the reader is familiar with the world of business either from firsthand experience in a senior leadership role or through coaching leaders at this level.

Our messages will be particularly relevant to coaches and leaders who have mastered the basic coaching skills and are now asking themselves the following questions:-

"So, where do I go from here?"

"How should my coaching skills evolve to suit a more challenging economic environment?"

"How do I deliver great 'bottom line' results for the business as well as building great personal relationships?"

"How and when would I risk breaking the rapport with my coachee in order to drive for results?"

"How do I make a contribution to moving forward the leadership consciousness in business without compromising my coaching ethics and values?"

.....and, of course, the BIG question:-

"So where were all the coaches when the banks went down?"

If these are questions you have asked yourself then the messages in this book will resonate with you. You will find answers to these questions in the FACTS coaching approach that the book describes and you will be challenged to convert these insights into practical coaching behaviours.

At 121partners, a leading coaching and leadership development consultancy, we have had to ask ourselves these questions because our clients are asking us these questions and our future business success depends upon us having credible and proven answers.

The book distils our 'front line' experience gained over many years. In the last eighteen months, we have developed our response to these questions and practised these skills in these challenging times with Board level leaders in FTSE250 organisations. It is a work in progress and there remains much to learn but we hope that, by sharing our collective experience now, we are making our own unique contribution to ensuring that coaching continues to play a mainstream role in the transformation of business performance as the new economic landscape unfolds.

John Blakey
Ian Day
December 2009

Prologue

Where were all the coaches when the banks went down? Pause for a moment to ponder this provocative question … what thoughts, reactions, ideas come up for you?

When we have posed this question at seminars and presentations, it has generated energetic conversations; it touches a nerve. For some, coaches were not being used pervasively enough in the financial sector to make a difference to the wider organisation. For others, they wonder about the level of

> *Where were all the coaches when the banks went down?*

detachment of the coaches who were coaching senior leaders in Lehmann Brothers, Northern Rock or RBS in the years leading up to 2009.

How much responsibility did coaches feel when they read newspaper headlines about individuals and organisations where they coached? Did they see the crisis coming yet feel powerless to influence events? How much accountability did they feel for the wider systematic outcomes beyond their individual coaching engagements? Could they have challenged more? Could they have held leaders more accountable on issues of ethics and limits and the wider consequences of their behaviour?

Or was it the consultants who were to blame … or the Non Executive Directors … or the Regulators? Maybe they should have 'blown the whistle' first? For others, the coaches were simply 'pocketing the money'; just like everyone else. They were getting their invoices in quickly before the dam

11

burst. They question the value of coaching. All the money that these banks must have spent on coaching - and what difference did it really make?

> *"Be the change you want to see in the world"* - Gandhi

For others, it makes them think about the non-directive nature of coaching. How could a non-directive intervention make any difference when the leaders involved were 'blind' to the situation? Should coaching techniques be different when the going gets tough or when there is an impending crisis? Where does the coach's responsibility lie when the organisation or individuals within fail? Where is the coach in this situation? What level of responsibility is it appropriate for the coach to take for this 'failure'? Who was the coach serving - the individual, the organisation, or themselves?

Also, what of contracting, confidentiality and supervision? Where were all of these coaching practices when the banks went down? What role did they play and what can we learn from the 'credit crunch' crisis that will improve these practices for the future?

From one simple question there are so many different views, so many reactions and so many perspectives. Yet the premise of this book is that when we get into new stages of the economic cycle and when the tide goes out and you see all the rubbish on the shore, every party has to ask themselves, *Where was I, what was I doing and what was my contribution? What am I learning from this?* As coaches, and as a coaching profession, we have to look at ourselves first. Yes, the consultants should have done something different. Yes, the leaders of the organisation should have done something different. Yes, the politicians should have done something different. All these parties could have been doing something different and could be blamed or not blamed for what went wrong depending upon your chosen prejudice.

But this book is about shining the light on ourselves, our coaching and our profession and asking, '*What are we going to learn?*' How might coaching best adapt to an environment in which these types of questions are being asked much more ruthlessly by the buyers of coaching services and how can we get our 'own house' in order and so inspire others to do likewise in their own, unique ways?

After all, isn't it Gandhi's words that we coaches most like to quote - '*Be the change you want to see in the world*'?

The Evolution of FACTS Coaching

Every profession evolves and matures. In a Darwinian sense, the professions of engineering and accountancy are probably the metaphorical equivalent of 'homo sapiens'. They have existed for hundreds of years and grown through every stage of the economic cycle, refining and adapting their practices.

When we present this topic to audiences that include psychologists, we poke a little fun and suggest that psychology is the 'chimpanzee' of the professions! Not everyone agrees with this metaphor but certainly psychology is a younger profession which is at an earlier stage of development than engineering or accountancy. It is still developing and changing rapidly as new theories and schools emerge - psychoanalytical, humanist, transpersonal, etc.

So where would coaching be on the evolutionary scale? Are we in fact the amoeba, the fish, the amphibian?

So where would coaching be on this evolutionary scale? Are we in fact the amoeba, the fish, the amphibian? It is easy to forget how young coaching is. Despite the pioneering work of the likes of Sir John Whitmore and Graham Alexander in the eighties, the International Coach Federation (ICF), the largest global professional body in coaching, was only formed in 1995. So, on this measure, the profession is a mere adolescent and nothing but a 'blip' on the evolutionary scale compared to even the profession of psychology.

We are being asked to coach for organisational 'needs' rather than for individual 'wants'.

Already, in that short span of time, the coaching profession has changed, developed and adapted. We have seen coaches specialising in specific tools and techniques, such as NLP and the Solutions Focus movement. We have seen the development of coaching supervision as the means of supporting coaches in their practice. We have seen a plethora of coaching bodies with various biases in terms of preferred coaching skills and competencies. Most of all, coaching has grown rapidly and become accepted as a mainstream leadership tool.

To realise this is to anticipate how much coaching will change in the next fifty years. It helps to open our minds to challenge all that we know about coaching today and to be prepared to change this and expand this as the profession matures. If anyone thinks we have got coaching 'sussed' with our competencies and accreditations and codes of ethics after only fifteen years, well, this book will be a 'wake up call' since it assumes that there is much more to learn and that even some of the current 'sacred cows' of coaching may yet be re-evaluated as the profession grows up.

At 121partners, we witnessed a marked shift in the demands of organisational buyers of coaching in the twelve to eighteen months up to the end of 2009 as the 'credit crunch' transformed the economic environment. We noticed that we were being asked to coach for organisational 'needs' rather than for individual 'wants'. Our programmes are now being validated against the business agenda of the organisation rather than the personal agendas of a particular talent pool. As this shift took place, we realised that it created a different emphasis in our style of coaching and challenged us to be creative in re-inventing our coaching presence to suit the new environment. In particular, we have had to focus upon the following skills to a much greater level than before:

Feedback - How does a coach give informative and inspirational feedback to leaders?

Accountability - How does a coach hold leaders accountable for commitments without blame or shame?

Challenge - How does a coach challenge leaders to step out of their comfort zones whilst staying credible and realistic in tough market conditions?

Tension - When is tension constructive? How can coaches practise creating and holding tension without risking burnout in key performers?

Systems Thinking - How can a coach stay sensitive to 'big picture' issues such as sustainability, ethics, diversity, and the environment without losing focus on 'bottom line' results?

Together, we have termed these skills the FACTS approach to coaching. We have joked with ourselves that maybe it is time for coaching to 'face the FACTS' if it is to stay relevant and credible in the new economic environment. Maybe this is one of the next steps on coaching's evolutionary ladder and, if it is, then how might this more results-focussed approach complement and build upon the relationship-based coaching that proliferated in the 'boom' years? To answer these questions, we need to explore in more detail the recent history of coaching and how the economic environment has shaped its development.

From Boom to Bust

Coaching has spent its formative years in the 'boom' times. During most of the decade up to 2008, we were stressing over the 'war for talent' and the biggest challenge for any organisation seemed to be attracting, retaining and developing the right people (Axelrod, Handfield-Jones & Welsh, May 2001). This seems a long time ago. In psychology there is a strong belief that the first five years of an individual's life are formative in terms of how that individual grows up in the world. If that is true of professions as well as individuals, then coaching was born and grew up in an environment that was unusual, with unprecedented levels of growth and an emphasis on executive coaching as a means of attracting and retaining top talent.

Coaching has spent its formative years in the 'boom' times.

When 121partners was first formed in 2003, one of our first FTSE250 clients was typical of this stage in the development of the coaching market. The company was a leading, global property management organisation which was growing rapidly and whose biggest problem was retaining top talent and preparing that talent for senior international appointments. 121partners was appointed to design and implement a leadership development programme for the 'Top 50' high potential leaders in Europe. The key objective of this programme was to focus on the individual, look at their career vision, help them make the next step and give them the feeling that the organisation cared for them.

How did such programmes, with their focus upon talent development, influence the development of the young coaching profession?

This was a programme about reward and recognition rather than a programme about performance improvement. It was all very personal - personal career visions, personal strengths, personal action plans. A very individualistic focus which reflected the 'boom' times - everything was expanding, opportunities were everywhere and the environment and the context were very different to that of now.

The programme was successful in that it reduced senior leadership attrition and facilitated key promotions. Both the individual and the organisation were happy.

But how did such programmes, with their focus upon talent development, influence the development of the young coaching profession? What skills did these programmes bring to the fore?

To answer these questions, it is interesting to reflect on the skills which the typical 'Introduction to Coaching' course of that time focussed upon. At 121partners, we have our own equivalent of this type of course; a one day 'coaching gym' that we have delivered to over three hundred senior leaders in different international cultures. This course is a 'wake up' call for all leaders who are conditioned by the 'command and control' environment prevalent in most large organisations. It injects a non-directive ethos and majors upon helping delegates develop their listening skills, their goal setting skills and their ability to ask powerful questions - all behaviours that are central to the ICF core competencies (ICF Core Competencies, 1999). Here is a selection of behaviours from the ICF core competencies that are examples of these skills:

> *Some would call these the 'soft' skills of coaching.*

- Shows genuine concern for the client's welfare and future

- Demonstrates respect for client's perceptions, learning style, personal being

- Attends to the client and the client's agenda, and not to the coach's agenda for the client

- Summarises, paraphrases, reiterates, mirrors back what client has said to ensure clarity and understanding

- Asks questions that reflect active listening and an understanding of the client's perspective

- Acknowledges the client for what they have done, not done, learned or become aware of since the previous coaching session.

Some would call these the 'soft' skills of coaching or the 'relationship building' skills of coaching. Take a moment to reflect on these behaviours and, if you are a coach or a leader trained in coaching skills, ask yourself how much these skills dominated your first understanding of how coaching is applied in a business context?

Now, whilst these behaviours are all a part of what makes for great coaching, there are some risks in making these the sole focus of a coaching approach. In our opinion, the risks are:-

- collusion

- irrelevance

- self-obsession

By collusion we mean that if a coach is simply asking questions, being non-judgemental and listening, then there is a risk that they might collude with the coachee, align 100% with their world view and fail to challenge or give feedback from a different perspective.

"How did we get here and what on earth has this got to do with the people that are paying me to be in front of this person right now?"

By irrelevance we mean that if the coach is always holding to the coachee's agenda then it is, in theory, possible that by the end of the second session they might be coaching on improving the coachee's golf swing rather than

21

anything that aligns with 'bottom line' business performance. Whilst this is a deliberately extreme example, how many of the coaches reading this book has ever had the following thought in the midst of a coaching session? - *"How did we get here and what on earth has this got to do with the people that are paying me to be in front of this person right now?"* Don't worry, you're probably not alone!

By self-obsession, we mean that these coaching skills risked fuelling the 'me, me, me' attitude that pervaded the previous fifteen years of economic growth but which many believe to have been a significant factor in the circumstances that led up to the 'credit crunch' problem. Self-centred financial traders, focussed solely upon their own rewards, took risks that in hindsight had unintended consequences on not just the wider organisation but the entire global banking system. It could be said that coaching 'focussed purely on the coachee's agenda' exacerbated this myopia rather than developing a greater awareness of the wider context in which each person and each organisation operated.

In the 'boom' years, when the focus was on using coaching to attract and retain talent, these risks were not critical. Indeed, many significant personal benefits arose from this style of coaching and there was a 'knock on' benefit to teams and organisations. But what happens when the environment suddenly shifts as it did at end of 2008? Even in the early months of 2008, leading head-hunters were calling an end to the war on talent (Logan, G, 2008). In this article, head-hunter firm Morgan McKinley, had found that new job vacancies in the financial services sector had dropped 65% between December 2007 and December 2008. Organisations shifted, almost overnight, from focussing upon attracting and retaining talent to shedding staff and looking at ways of maximising the performance of the lucky survivors that remained.

In this dramatically different environment, many organisations that had pursued coaching agendas with the best of intentions struggled to maintain an appropriate context for coaching. In our opinion this was due to an over-reliance on relationship based coaching skills combined with inadequate 'contracting' and insufficient involvement of wider business stakeholders.

Where do you go next when you have built a great relationship, but now you need to leverage this to deliver fantastic, 'bottom line' results?

One client of ours - a leading media organisation - who had trained all their sales managers through a typical 'Introduction to Coaching' course, noticed that much better relationships were then built between managers and staff, resulting in a reduction in attrition in the 'boom' years. However, in 2008, as they saw the first wave of the recession hit hard, they were struggling to convert these great relationships into 'bottom line' results and approached 121partners for advice. What was of even greater concern was that, in the absence of a clear way forward, some of the sales managers were reverting to a 'command and control' style of leadership. Whilst they knew this would undermine their newly developed, high trust relationships, they were tempted by the well proven ability of the 'command and control' approach to improve short term results.

Like many other organisations, they had completed 'phase 1' of their coaching agenda but were looking for a 'phase 2' approach to take them further forward and avoid a lurch backwards.

So where do you go next when you have built a great relationship with your coachee, based on trust and respect, but now you need to leverage this

23

to deliver fantastic 'bottom line' results? Where do you go as an HR Director when you need to convince the Board to sponsor a coaching programme in challenging times and they are struggling to make that link between coaching and the performance of the team and the business?

Well, the answer is not as far away as you might think. That same list of ICF core competencies that we referred to earlier also contains some very different behaviours that are listed below:-

- Positively confronts the client with the fact that he/she did not take agreed-upon actions

- Promotes client's self-discipline and holds the client accountable

- Creates a plan with results that are attainable, measurable, specific and have target dates

There is an 'edge' to these words that you can imagine driving results in a coaching dialogue.

- Challenges client's assumptions and perspectives to provoke new ideas and find new possibilities for action

- Is clear, articulate and direct in sharing and providing feedback

- Accesses own intuition and trusts one's inner knowing - 'goes with the gut'

- Is open to not knowing and takes risks.

Take a moment to reflect on these behaviours and ask yourself how familiar you are with these skills compared to the relationship building skills of coaching we listed earlier? You will notice phrases like 'positively confronts", 'promotes discipline', 'holds accountable', 'challenges perspectives', 'direct feedback', 'takes risks', 'goes with the gut'. You get a completely different energy from these words compared to those used earlier. There is an 'edge' to these words that you can imagine driving results in a coaching dialogue.

These skills are not used instead of the relationship building skills but they expand on these and leverage them to improve performance. In the new economic times, we suggest that these 'edgy' coaching skills will be crucial if coaching is to stay relevant to the needs of the buyers of coaching. For it is these skills that will enable managers and coaches to get more out of the people

> *In the hands of a confident, experienced coach or leader these skills could be positive and impactful.*

around them without sacrificing high trust personal relationships or reverting to a 'command and control' mind set.

The FACTS approach is a response to the challenge of converting great coaching relationships to great 'bottom line' results. It is an approach that both leaders and coaches can use to take their coaching skills to the next level and provide an 'edge' to their coaching presence, focussing upon the five core skills of feedback, accountability, challenge, tension and systems thinking.

These are more advanced coaching skills that can only be mastered once you have built the firm foundation of an open and trusting relationship. Any of these approaches could risk breaking the rapport in a coaching

25

relationship if they were practised in the wrong way, at the wrong time and with the wrong motivation. But in the hands of a confident, experienced coach or leader these skills will be positive and impactful.

Consider Figure 1. If a coach spends 100% of his/her time deploying relationship building skills (the extreme left hand side on the diagram), there will be a very strong relationship, even a friendship, with high levels of rapport, trust and empathy, but potentially no results. If the coach focusses on the extreme right hand side of the diagram there will be high levels of feedback, accountability, challenge and tension but, without the foundation of a strong relationship, the coaching is unlikely to last. So this is not a 'black and white' situation, but it is about the proportion of time that a coach uses their relationship building skills compared to their results focussed skills.

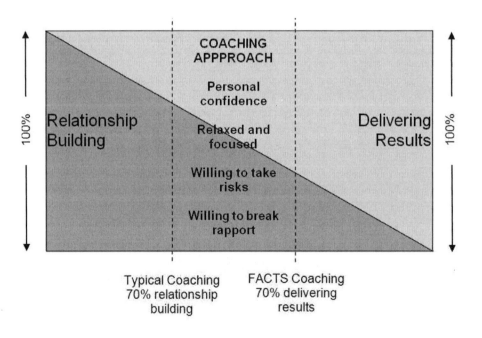

Figure 1

In the boom times, coaching was typically 70% relationship focussed and 30% results focussed. This was appropriate at a time when the 'war for talent' was at its height. The reward, recognition and retention of key players in organisations were crucial. The indirect cost of losing these key people was significant, and the direct cost of hiring and on-boarding new talent focussed attention onto retention. So coaching around the personal agenda was appropriate.

However, times have changed and the challenges of 2009 onwards require a greater business focus rather than person focus. A purchaser of coaching requires more results orientation with, say, 70% of the coaching work focussed on results and 30% focussed upon relationship building.

The over reliance on relationship building skills encourages coaches to view rapport as sacrosanct.

The 70/30 example is a simplification of the reality of each unique coaching relationship. However, the point of the example is to encourage coaches to think about where they might be on this spectrum with their coachees as the coaching sessions develop and deepen and as the external circumstances change.

For some coachees, an 80% relationship based focus would still be appropriate because of their personalities and the way that person 'gets from A to B'. For other clients, the coach might start with an 80% relationship focus in the first coaching session but, later, once the trust and rapport has been secured, they might shift to an 80% results focus in the fourth session. This is a dynamic balance and the purpose of the FACTS approach is to help coaches explore this dynamic, become more aware of it and therefore make more conscious choices as to how their coaching presence is experienced.

The FACTS approach requires coaches to 'stretch' and be willing to risk their 'friendship' with the coachee in order to achieve results. This requires a shift in emphasis for coaches and coach training courses. The over reliance on relationship building skills encourages coaches to view rapport as sacrosanct but in challenging times, when business survival is at the fore, there needs to be a shift to an approach where results and return on investment for the business is not only valued but seen as paramount by the coach.

To do this, a coach needs high levels of personal confidence (absolute belief that this approach is the best and will work and have the skills to support the belief), a willingness to take risks (if results are not achieved the coaching will end), and a willingness to break rapport (to risk the 'friendliness' of the relationship in favour of results).

In this context, we believe it is time for coaches to face the FACTS!

Key Learning Points

- It is easy to forget that coaching is a young profession and, because of this, to realise that it will change dramatically in the next fifty years

- Coaching 'grew up' in the boom years and this backdrop focussed coaches on their 'relationship building' skills

- In more challenging economic times, a shift to focus upon coaching skills that 'deliver results' is appropriate

- These skills were always present in coaching, in theory, but have not been practised as widely as might now need to be the case

- The key is to find a dynamic balance between the 'building relationships' and 'delivering results' skills in any coaching relationship.

The Zone of Uncomfortable Debate

In the previous chapter we discussed how, in the short lifetime of the coaching industry, the world has gone through an economic cycle which has necessitated the evolution of coaching skills which are sharper and more results focussed. In this chapter we start to look at how this is achieved.

Let us consider how conversations and interactions take place and look at a model developed by Professor Cliff Bowman at Cranfield University (Bowman, 1995). Consider Figure 2 - the centre of the diagram represents the core of the issue which, once discussed, provides the key to making a breakthrough; moving understanding to the next level, or moving an idea forward,

> *The model proposes that people in an interaction must work through the ZOUD, rather than avoid it, to make progress.*

or unblocking a problem, or resolving an argument. Around this are two concentric layers, firstly the 'zone of comfortable debate' and, secondly, the 'zone of uncomfortable debate' (ZOUD). When two people interact, the conversation begins in the zone of comfortable debate, and then, depending on the situation, may or may not move into the ZOUD. How individuals respond when in this uncomfortable zone will determine if the issue at hand is resolved and the people involved in the conversation get to the heart of the matter, or whether they avoid the tension and move back into the comfortable zone. The model proposes that people in an interaction must work through the ZOUD, rather than avoid it, to make progress.

31

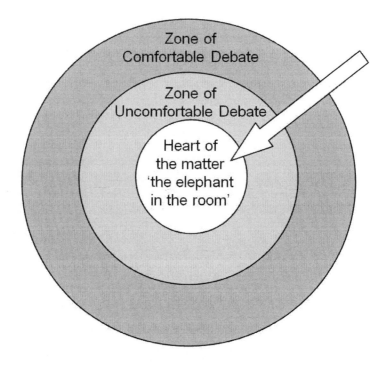

Figure 2

When an interaction begins between two or more people there is typically a period of small talk, rapport building, developing an understanding of common ground, etc. This is where the conversation is nice, it's easy, it feels relaxed and there's not a lot of tension. The people are chatting about easy, obvious things - for example, catching up on news and gossip, what has happened since the people last met, and common interests such as sport and family. This stage of the conversation is very straightforward and is the zone of comfortable debate.

If this conversation is to be more than a social chat, there is usually a matter at the heart of the discussion. The parties have come together for a purpose - to agree action, to make a decision, to resolve a problem, etc. To achieve this, a social comfortable conversation is not sufficient and, to get to the heart of the issue, the conversation must move to a zone of uncomfortable debate. In this zone there is a feeling of increased tension and the pressure starts to build as the parties may disagree and may not see 'eye-to-eye'. What often happens is that the individuals feel the tension, find it uncomfortable and, fearing the pressure will permanently damage the relationship, the conversation moves back out to the zone of comfortable debate. The tension is diffused and the rapport is maintained, but the matter at hand has not been resolved. The core issue is still the same and no movement has taken place. To resolve the issue, the conversation must stay in the ZOUD and the parties work through it to uncover differences in understanding, assumptions, motives, etc. By sustaining the ZOUD people can move to the heart of the issue

Perhaps we don't want to make the elephant angry in case it damages the whole house.

and resolve it permanently and then move on to a new topic.

The heart of the issue is a bit like having an 'elephant in the room'. Here is something enormous that is taking up significant space. However, the 'elephant' is not dealt with directly as it is such a big and difficult thing. Perhaps we don't want to make the elephant angry in case it damages the whole house, or maybe we are too polite to comment on it. What happens is that people find innovative and creative ways to move around the 'elephant', to manage it and live with it. Until they face up to the fact that there is actually an 'elephant in the room' and try to remove it directly, the situation will remain unchanged. Facing up to this fact and dealing with it is going to be uncomfortable - there are risks involved so this is like entering the ZOUD.

So what is the connection between this model of general communication and coaching? The connection is that coaches often work in difficult areas of personal development. If these areas were simple to understand and easy to resolve, the person would not need a coach, they would have simply done it themselves. Often coaching is about holding a mirror up and showing the coachee something they do not want to see and have avoided up to now. Coaching is about challenging assumptions, examining habits, overcoming barriers and embedding change. For this to work the coach must feedback, challenge and hold the coachee accountable and be prepared to go into the ZOUD and hold the tension until the 'heart of the matter' is opened up and resolved. All the components of the FACTS approach require the coach to enter the ZOUD more often, more skilfully and with total belief this is in the best long term interest of the coaching relationship.

> *So what is the connection between this model of general communication and coaching?*

There are risks associated with this; through the tension of the ZOUD the coaching relationship could be irreparably damaged. The coach may feel that there is a risk of rapport being lost and so releases the tension moving the conversation back to the benign zone of comfortable debate. So there is an elaborate dance of dialogue that takes place around the core issue. There is one step into the ZOUD and then a step back into the zone of comfortable debate, and the dance continues without addressing the issues. A more constructive strategy is for the coach to stick with the tension and accept it as positive and constructive. This uncomfortable feeling is inevitable and essential to get to the heart of the matter, and so the coach needs to be confident to stay in the ZOUD and confront challenging issues.

Some coaches may have difficulty with this concept. As a coach you believe you are there to serve the coachee, holding them in unconditional positive regard, with all your coaching training emphasising the importance of rapport and not being directive. Sometimes, wanting to be the peacemaker, a coach may feel the need to maintain harmony and find 'common ground' and so diffuse the tension by going back into the zone of comfortable debate and creating innovative strategies to approach the subject in a different way that is less tense. The challenge for the coach is to

At the heart of this is the importance of a coach holding direct communication as opposed to directive communication.

stay in the ZOUD. At the heart of this is the importance of a coach holding direct communication as opposed to directive communication.

So what will enable a coach to enter and work with the ZOUD? This is about the belief of the coach. High potential individuals are typically robust and able to hold strong debate. The coach is there to serve the coachee and the organisation sponsoring the coaching, and so any intervention will be designed to be positive and constructive. The coach feels tension and has the confident belief that this will lead to a breakthrough. The tension can be diffused by the coachee who taps into this energy and makes the shift. If the coaching relationship is built on solid relationship skills, it will be strong enough to sustain that amount of tension and benefit from facing rather than avoiding the heart of the issue.

35

The concept of the ZOUD and being comfortable to enter the ZOUD as a coach is fundamental to all the components of the FACTS approach. Whether it be in delivering feedback, holding accountability, challenging or creating constructive tension, a coach using the FACTS approach will need to be aware of the ZOUD and be able to consciously enter into it when the situations demands. In the subsequent chapters, we will explore each of the FACTS components but this foundation of the ZOUD awareness and confidence will remain constant throughout.

ZOUD Exercise

- Reflect on a time when have you entered the ZOUD - what happened?

- When have you held the tension, and when have you diffused it - what does this tell you?

- What core assumptions do you hold about tension and the importance of rapport?

- What is the difference between direct and directive communication?

- What are the conditions that will enable you as a coach to enter the ZOUD and work within it?

Key Learning Points

- Most conversations take place in the 'Zone of Comfortable Debate'

- People avoid the ZOUD ('Zone of Uncomfortable Debate') because it feels tense, uncomfortable and out of control

- To achieve results, both coach and coachee need to feel comfortable to enter the ZOUD and tackle the 'heart of the issue'

- All of the components of the FACTS coaching approach involve being able to sustain the ZOUD with a coachee.

Feedback

Feedback Theory

The first skill of the FACTS approach that needs to be sharpened is that of giving effective feedback. A coaching session is like a laboratory where the coachee experiments by trying out new behaviours and reflecting on past experiences. The coach will interact with the coachee and observe and react to many behaviours, some of which the coachee is aware of and some of which the coachee is unaware of. In this laboratory, the coach is a great source of feedback by providing information about how the coachee's action, words, tone of voice and silences are interpreted. There is the assumption that, whilst in the coaching session, the coachee will display behaviour that is typical of how he/she behaves outside of the coaching session and when interacting with people on an everyday basis. This is typically the case if there is a high level of trust built out of strong rapport and so the coachee is at ease, relaxed and acting as he/she normally would.

The coach is a great source of feedback by providing information about how the coachee's action, words, tone of voice and silences are interpreted.

Two of the largest coaching bodies have identified feedback as fundamental to the effectiveness of coaching. The ICF identifies feedback as a core competence relating to direct communication which mandates that a coach 'is clear, articulate and direct in sharing and providing feedback' (ICF Core Competencies, 2009). The Association for Coaching (AC) states that fostering independence in the coachee is a core competency and one of the three points within this is that 'the coach monitors improvement in the coachee and feeds this back as evidence of development' (AC Core Competencies, 2005).

Although feedback is integral in coaching competency models, it seems forgotten and hidden behind other more obvious coaching behaviours. Some coaches think that providing feedback is outside of their role and this may be for a number of reasons. One reason is that feedback is an advanced skill and not often covered in depth in coaching courses or books. Many courses and books work with the GROW model (Whitmore, Coaching for Performance, 2002) and cover questioning, listening, summarising, and goal setting. These are all valuable skills that are the fundamentals of a coach's tool kit, but the courses and books often omit feedback skills. Another reason may be that the non-directive coach believes that the coachee should discover the feedback directly from another source when outside the coaching session. The coach may consider that providing feedback is like giving advice and so may be a directive step, preventing the coachee from having the opportunity to learn and seek feedback for him/herself.

> *Badly delivered feedback can be as harmful as no feedback at all.*

A third reason is that providing feedback is incredibly difficult to do effectively and can come across as clumsy and ineffective. Badly delivered feedback can be as harmful as no feedback at all. We can all think of something that we said that was misinterpreted and taken as a negative

40

comment, despite a heartfelt positive intention. Comments that are misinterpreted can lead to an emotional reaction that is very powerful, and so we remember these events vividly.

Because of these reasons, a coach may avoid providing feedback. However, if a coach does not provide feedback or provides vague feedback then the coachee will not become aware of a 'blind spot' and continue with habitual behaviour and approaches that may not lead to the desired outcome.

The additional perspective provided through feedback is an invaluable tool to aid the coachee's development.

In normal day-to-day interactions, there are many things that prevent effective feedback. Consider how often, and in what situations, you give and receive feedback. It is likely that feedback is not forthcoming, is infrequent, and, more often than not, occurs when something has gone wrong. Respect for the person, status, relationship, organisational politics, and politeness may result in feedback being edited or limited and so losing its value. Over time, feedback may not be sought out and thus only forthcoming when problems occur.

Through the privileged and unique position in the 'laboratory of learning', the coach can add a great wealth of information and feedback to the coachee. The coachee can be free of all of the conditions relating to typical interactions and relationships, the coach has no emotional attachment, there are no organisational politics and the coach is not attached to the outcome. If the coach is confident and free to risk breaking rapport with the coachee, the additional perspective provided through feedback is an

41

invaluable tool to aid the coachee's development. It is as if the coach is holding a mirror up to the coachee and showing him/her what other people see.

Feedback in Practice

Effective feedback requires both process and skills. We will outline a simple process to provide effective feedback but before we review, let us consider the intention of the person delivering the feedback. A 'person centred' or 'Rogerian' (Rogers, 2004) coach will hold the belief that a coachee has within themselves vast resources for development and has the capacity to grow and they will have unconditional positive regard towards

Effective feedback requires both process and skills.

the coachee. Based on this solid foundation, the intention of any feedback will be positive. Feedback will be constructive and positively contribute towards the achievement of the coachee's objectives. This does not prevent the feedback from being challenging and at times difficult for the coachee to accept. However, the intention of the coach when delivering feedback will always be based on the coachee achieving his/her full potential through awareness of their 'blind spots'.

The intention of the coach can be different to the intention of other people providing feedback. In a workplace, feedback is often delivered by a boss to a subordinate or by a client to a supplier. In these cases, there is not always a positive intention. Typically, feedback is given when something has gone wrong and emotions are 'running high'. It can be like an angry parent telling off a child. Maybe this is why we have negative associations when thinking of feedback as the feelings and memories are linked to our childhood experiences at home or at school and when 'learning the ropes' at work?

Feedback from a coach is very different, and the coach should view it so. The feedback is a gift to aid self-awareness and to reduce 'blind spots'. The coach has no ego or status in this situation, and provides feedback on how behaviour is seen and how the coach interprets the actions of the coachee. Feedback on how the coach felt - what he/she thought and the assumptions made by the coach - are valuable sources of information. If the coach is not willing to share these, then the coachee is destined to remain unaware of how he/she is perceived by others. The role of a coach is to create the conditions where growth is encouraged and facilitated and so feedback is essential.

> *The coach has no ego or status in this situation, and provides feedback on how behaviour is seen.*

There are many models for providing effective feedback. One which we use regularly with our clients has the following stages: what is observed; what is the impact; invite input; establish action plan; as a way of making sure that feedback is effective as possible. For more details on this model, refer to Appendix 1.

Preparation and Practice

An important aspect of feedback is preparation; preparing what to feedback and how. This is the same with any new skill such as learning to drive a car - you need practice. In the same way feedback requires preparation and practice to maximise impact and effectiveness. In time the preparation needed may be just a couple of seconds of mental rehearsal but at the start you will need to think through all the stages of the feedback model.

Example

You are in the third session and you've just given the coachee this feedback: *"I've noticed that in each of the last two sessions you haven't completed the actions that you said you were going to."*…. (Stage 1 –observed) …. *"so when we get to that point again where we are agreeing actions, I lack belief that you will see them through"*… (Stage 2 – impact)… *"How do you see this and what can we do to improve the situation?"*… (Stage 3 – Invite Input + Stage 4 – Action)

Application

This approach to feedback can be used in a number of ways during a coaching session. For example:

- What the coach observes during the session such as what is said, energy levels, avoidance, what has been done in-between sessions, etc.

- Reflecting on past events. The coachee may be describing a situation that has happened and so reflecting on the past to inform future actions. While exploring what happened, and who said what, feedback can be used to provide an insight into what the coach heard and how he/she interpreted the actions and to ask the coachee if the possible interpretations had been considered and what to do in the future.

- Practicing for the future. Another application is relating to future actions as the coachee may be imagining a future situation, may be role playing or using an 'empty chair' exercise (Simkin & Yontef,

1993). The coach can provide valuable input as the coachee rehearses new behaviours, like a theatrical director on stage working with an actor to perfect his/her performance.

Feedback Exercise

The exercise below is an opportunity to practicing giving feedback. Consider a coaching session; the coachee has identified a personal goal of throwing a ball over his shoulder into a bin. As a coach you must give the coachee feedback to help develop awareness and to achieve his objective.

Work through the stages:

- Observed – what was seen/what happened (specific, factual, descriptive, non-judgemental, 'the act not the actor')

- Impact – what assumptions did you (or others) make as a result, how did you feel, what are the consequences?

- Invite input – 'how do you see this?'

- Action – what should be done? Future focussed and constructive (something can be done)

An example of poor feedback from the coach in this situation:

- *"You missed, that was not very good"*

- *"I don't think you're motivated to achieve this objective"*

- *"I guess you see it the same way as me"*

- *"Try again"*

An example of more effective feedback from the coach in this situation:

- *"The ball landed 12 inches in front of the bin and to the left"*

- *"I think that if you adjust your throw you will achieve your objective"*

- *"How did it feel to you and what do you think you can do differently next time?"*

- *"Ok then, try throwing the ball a little harder by bringing your arm down further as you throw and let's review again".*

Case Study - Feedback

David is a senior manager with a large UK based organisation. As part of a large scale leadership development programme, David is receiving five two hour coaching sessions. The purpose of the coaching is to embed the learning from the 'taught' elements of the programme and to personalise the development so that it will focus on David's key areas of development. The contracting process has taken place and personal development objectives have been agreed between David, his line manager and human resources director.

The prime area that David has identified for his development is influence and impact and, as he put it, he wishes to *'establish himself as a respected member of the team, be recognised as an expert and be well informed, with a sensible view point, in one-to-one discussions and in meetings'*. David identified the measures of success for this objective as being *'people taking on board what I say, that I come across as confident when conveying opinions and points of view and there is an increase in the number of people asking for my advice and opinion.'*

David is a very experienced and intelligent person and during your discussions it is evident that David's style when communicating has a significant impact on his ability to make a positive impact and be seen as confident and persuasive. When David talks he always looks down at his note pad on the desk and does not make any eye contact at all, the volume of his voice reduces and at times it is difficult to hear what he is saying. This

47

occurs throughout your first meeting as we build rapport and work through his development objectives in detail.

It is now the second coaching meeting - what approach would you take?

The FACTS Response

We are back in the laboratory of learning as the coach develops hypotheses to test out in the coaching session. The key is for the coach to prepare and do some scenario planning. The hypotheses could be:

- This may be a product of the first coaching session and not typical of David's everyday style.

- This is typical and so the coach should be prepared to provide David with feedback.

The second meeting starts as the first meeting ended. David's communication style is exactly the same - he looks down every time he talks and it is difficult to hear him. As a coach you conclude that the second hypothesis is correct. Once David has reported on progress on the actions he agreed following the first meeting, the coach reviews the objectives to check relevance and find out if priorities have changed.

David confirms that influencing and communication is still at the heart of his areas for development and this provides the coach with the link to provide feedback on what has been observed *"You identified the objective of improving your impact and influence and I would like to give you some feedback, I've noticed that every time you talk you look down at your note book, and then there is no eye contact."* This is a clear statement of fact without judgement or value statements. For this, preparation is key; the coach can 'script' the opening statement for this hypothesis in advance to ensure that it is neutral whilst being clear.

The coach follows on with *"When you do this I can't hear you very well, the energy level seems to drop, I feel that you may not be confident about what you are saying and what you are saying loses impact"*. Through this the coachee has an insight into how his style is perceived and interpreted by other people.

The coach then invites David's response with an open question *"what do you think about my assumption?"*

David agrees with the interpretation and, through reflection of how other people may perceive this, concludes that this has a significant impact on his ability to communicate effectively with influence and confidence.

Through this process David is aware and motivated to take action. He is aware of a blind spot and wants to take action to change. The benefit to him is the achievement of his goal, which is to be noticed.

The coach feels that it is appropriate to challenge David to take action and says *"let's try an exercise - talk to me for five minutes about your most recent holiday and maintain eye contact as you speak."*

In the safe environment of the coaching room David accepts the challenge. However, he still looks down at his note book even though there is nothing written on the open pages. The coach reaches over and takes the note book away, closes it and puts it on the other side of the table. David smiles as he recognises why the coach has done this and continues talking for four minutes.

The coach pauses the exercise and initiates a de-brief by asking *"how was that?"*

A detailed conversation follows with great openness and depth of thought from David. An action plan is agreed and the session ends.

During this coaching session David received feedback and challenge. The 'elephant in the room' has been identified and awareness and action has followed. Through preparation by the coach, the feedback was constructive and future focussed. David faced the FACTS and moved on.

Key Learning Points

- Coaching is about developing self-awareness and feedback develops the awareness of the coachee

- The coaching session is often an example of the coachee's typical behaviour when interacting with other people

- Feedback from the coach provides an invaluable additional perspective to uncover any 'blind spots' the coachee may have

- Feedback needs to be timely with potential to be acted on

- The intention of the coach is positive and orientated to working with the coachee to achieve positive objectives so feedback is a gift.

Accountability

Accountability Theory

Next in our understanding of the FACTS approach is 'A' for accountability. To understand the role of accountability in the FACTS approach then it is important to reflect upon the wider attitude towards accountability in society at large. Events such as the public reaction to the UK's MP expenses scandal and the disgust at the financial industry bonus culture seem to suggest that there is a shift in attitudes going on in the wider world. What trends are driving this change?

First, technology and the internet are making information more freely available to a global audience in an uncensored format. In parallel, the 'Generation Y' population is growing up with a less deferent attitude towards those in authority; they are less likely to give people respect based on a job title alone and have higher expectations of standards of behaviour in our worldly institutions.

When these trends are combined with a deep recession then the public tolerance for excess, greed, elitism and privilege reaches a new low. The furore over the UK's MP expenses scandal in 2009 demonstrated this vividly. In this example, the vast majority of MP's had not done anything illegal, or even broken any policy rule, yet still the public vented

The public expected each individual to apply their own personal moral code and act in a manner that would stand this test.

unprecedented anger onto those who they saw as failing to meet their accountabilities as public servants. The public expected each individual to apply their own personal moral code and act in a manner that would stand this test. Few passed this test and, as a result, the public lost further respect for this brand of leader.

What is the impact of this shift on the coaching profession?

If the coaching profession is to anticipate this trend rather than react to it then coaches would be acting as strong 'agents of accountability' in their work with business leaders and their teams. We too would be less tolerant and less accepting of coachees who fall short in areas where they have responsibilities and commitments to uphold.

Exactly what is it that coaches would be holding coachees accountable for whilst staying true to a 'non-judgemental' mindset? Cleary, commitment to agreed actions by the coachee are a simple example. Beyond this, the coach can also hold the coachee accountable for any discrepancy between words, feelings, body language and actions. For example, a coach might find themselves observing *"when you were describing what you did in that situation, I noticed that your eyes looked to the ground and I remembered how you have previously expressed strong negative opinions about leaders who adopt similar practices. What is going on here?"*

The coach can also hold the coachee accountable to commitments they have made implicitly by being leaders in a wider organisational context. For example, most organisations have a clear mission statement, strategy, set of values and corporate social responsibility agenda. In the FACTS approach, the coach makes it their business to understand this context in detail so that the coachee can be held accountable to the collective body of which they are part. For example, a coach may observe *"I am aware that one of the values of this*

54

organisation is 'honesty'. You are clearly involved in a situation here where you don't feel that everyone involved is 'walking the talk' regarding this value. What are you going to do to be honest about this with others?"

In the good times, maybe we were tempted to accept our coachees and their failings too easily, 'to meet them where they are at' and take the path of least resistance by 'making allowances', 'giving some slack' and 'letting go'. Whilst these skills remain part of the experienced coach's toolkit, the FACTS approach encourages coaches to shift the balance and act with courage to hold accountable the most powerful senior leaders if, in the moment, this is what the situation calls for.

> *In the good times, maybe we were tempted to accept our coachees and their failings too easily.*

Accountability in Practice

Having explored how accountability is shifting in the new economic climate and its impact upon the coaching profession, let us explore this further via a simple 'thought experiment'.

Figure 3 shows a graph of the share price trend of the major banks prior to, and during, the economic crisis.

Figure 3

Those banks all had CEO's who were responsible for leading them into and during that crisis. Whatever the rights and wrongs of it, there was considerable public anger at the greed and apparent lack of accountability of senior leaders during that period. Did any of these leaders have a coach in the run up to the 'credit crunch'? Who knows? However, in this 'thought experiment', we are going to ask you to imagine that you were a coach to one of those leaders!

You have been contracted to coach the CEO of a major bank for four sessions of two hours and you are now about to start the second session at his luxurious and intimidating offices in central London. The second coaching session just happens to coincide with the day that the bank's share price reached its peak; happy days! The CEO arrives for the session a fashionably ten minutes late and looks to you to take the lead:

"How have you got on with the actions you committed to take from our first coaching session?" you boldly venture.

Did any of these leaders have a coach in the run up to the 'credit crunch'? Who knows?

"Could you just remind me what those actions were?" he replies.

"Well, you were going to speak to your HR Director to review the bonus scheme for senior managers".

"Look, I've really been rather busy." he replies sharply, *"I've been tied up with some really important pension negotiations and I just haven't had the time to do any of those actions."*

So, as the coach, what would you do now?

In front of you is the Chief Executive of one of the most powerful organisations in the country. The organisation is paying you a princely sum to coach the CEO and he walks into the second session and this is the coaching dilemma that he presents you with.

Part of you is screaming to let it go and not risk the rapport and relationship that you have so carefully been building. This is partly because you believe this is good coaching and partly because you have a lot to lose if you upset this powerful CEO; such as your reputation, your fees, and your prospect of any future work in the account. Another part of you is urging you to be brave and hold him accountable, to explore the precedent that is being set and to not become just another fawning acolyte. You are wishing that you had been more explicit about accountability in your initial contracting session with him.

> *Part of you is screaming to let it go and not risk the rapport and relationship that you have so carefully been building.*

Now, review the 'building relationships' coaching skills and 'delivering results' coaching skills presented earlier in the first chapter. Use these to consider the range of the possible responses to this coaching dilemma, all of which could meet the various ICF coaching standards. Where do your responses sit? For example, a possible response might be to say to him *"That's ok; I understand you have been very busy. Let's focus on what you want to get out of today's session."* This would be pitched towards the 'building relationships' end of the spectrum. On the other hand, another possible response would be *"You told me you were committed to taking action. So what happened?"* This would be pitched at the 'delivering results' end of the spectrum. This is shown in Figure 4.

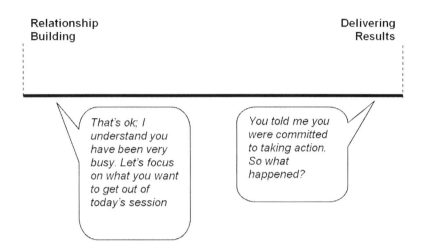

Relationship Building

Delivering Results

That's ok; I understand you have been very busy. Let's focus on what you want to get out of today's session

You told me you were committed to taking action. So what happened?

Figure 4

Most of all, ask yourself if your response would have been different if you knew that in six months time your coachee would be splashed all over the newspapers, pilloried for all that is wrong in the financial services sector and having brought the company to its knees. What sort of coach would you have been proud to have been when this bank went down? How would you contract to have permission to be this sort of coach with all of your coachees going forward?

> *What sort of coach would you have been proud to have been when this bank went down?*

Accountability Exercise

Working in a pair or in small groups, consider the dilemma presented in the previous section. On a flip chart draw a horizontal straight line and mark one end of the line 'Building Relationships' and the other end of the line

'Delivering Results'. Brainstorm all the possible coaching responses to the dilemma; check these against the ICF core competencies and plot each of them on this line to the degree to which you think they represent 'Building Relationships' or 'Delivering Results'.

Listen to other people's responses and use these to benchmark where you would position yourself between the two extremes and how this compares to others. Ask yourself if you are comfortable with your current position. If not, what is the adjustment you would like to make? If you are working with fellow coaches, coach each other on this topic, identifying the underlying factors that drive your decision making in these situations and examining if these are in the best service of your coaching presence and impact.

There are many possible responses - experiment with these and have fun going to the extremes as well as exploring the 'middle ground'. Don't stop until you have at least five possible answers plotted on your flip chart.

Case Study – Holding Accountability

You are working with Peter, the Managing Director of an international company, who has recently been appointed to his first role based outside of his 'home' country. Peter is now leading a large business services operation in Asia based out of Singapore and has requested help with adapting to some of the cross cultural challenges in his role. You have contracted to carry out four telephone coaching sessions and a FACTS based coaching agreement (see Appendix 2) has been agreed with the individual and his line manager who is based in the UK.

In your first session, Peter established that one of his goals was to become more aware of his personal values so that he could use these to guide him to display consistent, confident behaviour in a complex, cross cultural setting. As his coach, you carried out a simple 'values elicitation' exercise and it became clear that his No.1 value was 'openness'. It is now the second session and you are working on a more practical topic where the MD is planning a reorganisation of his business and seeking your support as to the best means of achieving this change efficiently and effectively.

In the midst of the session, Peter starts to describe how he is planning to communicate the reorganisation in different ways to different groups of staff, giving some more information than others and, in some cases, deliberately avoiding difficult questions to ensure that he does not upset vested interests. As a FACTS coach, what do you do next?

The FACTS Response

At the next appropriate pause, you decide to reflect back to Peter all that he has just been saying regarding the communication exercise and check that you have understood this correctly. He confirms this to be the case. You then choose to hold Peter accountable to the outcomes of the values elicitation exercise completed in the first session by saying *"Peter, I am feeling some discomfort here because in the first session you identified that 'openness' was your No.1 value and now you are describing to me a communication approach that sounds like it is guarded and closed".*

Peter's eyes look to the window and he takes a moment to think. *"Mmmm, yes, you have a point there. I am being closed and guarded in this situation but I am really worried about the consequences of being open with everyone around this message".*

"Well, let's explore those consequences a little more" you venture *"What is the worst that could happen if you are fully open with communicating the message to all parties regarding this reorganisation?".*

Peter: *"I guess there could be some very difficult conversations, a lot of emotion, people threatening to resign and a drop in morale that could damage performance".*

Coach: *"And what is the best that could happen if you are fully open with communicating the message to all parties?"*

Peter: *"The best that could happen is that people understand the business need for why I am doing what I am doing and they respect the openness with which I am communicating and, despite some short term concerns, in the medium term this builds a much stronger ethos and performance in the business".*

Coach: *"So here you are - someone who prides themselves on being very open yet recognising that you might choose to compromise this value in these circumstances because you don't know how people will respond. That's difficult".*

Peter: *"Yes, and I am just remembering that my No. 2 value after openness was courage. It does not honour this value either if I avoid difficult conversations in order to seek a 'quiet life' in the short term. I can't believe I was thinking of going down that path. It is just that, in this new and different environment, I am struggling to stay true to myself and I keep 'second guessing' what everyone else's reactions might be to what I do and say".*

Coach: *"It is a tough call and you are even more 'out of control' of the outcomes because you don't yet fully understand the cultural norms around here. All you are left with is knowing what your own values are. I am holding you accountable to these right now because you shared them with me in the first session".*

Peter: *"Yes, it's a fair cop. I am glad that you have done this because there is no one else around me right now with whom I can have this conversation. I was in danger of 'sleepwalking' down a path that I would have regretted in a few months time. Thank you for 'holding my feet to the fire'. "*

Key Learning Points

- Society at large has become less tolerant of leaders who do not meet minimum standards of accountability, particularly in tough times

- Coaches can anticipate and adapt to this trend by acting as stronger 'agents of accountability' in their coaching relationships

- Coachees should be held accountable not just for taking actions but for broader holistic responsibilities

- Holding the coachee accountable requires the coach to risk disrupting the relationship and rapport they have built

- The coach's approach to accountability is best agreed with the coachee 'up front' in the initial contracting session.

Challenge

Challenge Theory

With the FACTS approach, feedback and accountability can both be challenging behaviours but one is focussed upon learning from the past and the other is focussed upon delivering in the present – neither is solely future-focussed. The distinctive nature of the 'C' in FACTS is that it stands for challenging the coachee in terms of their future performance and their future potential. How does a coach most effectively challenge to unlock the future potential of the coachee?

Challenge is a word that means different things to different people. To some it is a word that has negative connotations. People may have experienced challenging behaviours that de-motivated them and undermined their confidence in the past. An old boss who constantly challenged you to 'pull your socks up' or to 'sort it out' or to 'get your act together' is not often remembered

How does a coach most effectively challenge to unlock the future potential of the coachee?

fondly! This style of challenge was often simply a means of criticising others, maintaining authority over them and was based on a belief that people would always be the same and would never meet or exceed expectations because they would never change.

Contrast this to a coach who has 100% unconditional belief in the totality of the coachee's greatness; a coach who sees more potential in the coachee than they see in themselves; a coach who is committed to supporting them to realise this potential. A challenge that comes from someone with this mind-set will be received very differently from that of a critical and over-bearing mentor.

In the 'good times', even if a coach had belief in the coachee's greatness, maybe they would have been tempted to dilute their challenges or to accept the coachee's own limiting belief in themselves. If the coachee was happy with themselves, and the organisation was happy too, then why bother 'rocking the boat' by asking this talented individual to stretch even further, to get out of their comfort zone and become the true 'star' that they could be? Maybe acceptance replaced effective challenge whereas, in difficult times, we all have more reason to dig deeper and unlock the potential which has been left untapped during the complacency of the 'good times'.

We are encouraging coaches to unlearn the negative definitions of the word challenge.

In the FACTS approach the dictionary definition of challenge that we choose to use is 'a test of one's abilities or resources in a demanding but stimulating undertaking'. Contrast this with other dictionary definitions such as 'take exception to' or 'a demand to explain, justify', or 'to demand something due or rightful', these phrases have all the negative connotations that can spook coaches into not using challenge fully as part of their coaching presence. We are encouraging coaches to unlearn the negative definitions of the word challenge, and to embrace fully the positive definition and build this type of challenge more fully into their practice.

Challenge in Practice

Like feedback, effective challenge needs to be practised and may feel a little 'pushy' at first. For example, as a coach can you imagine saying to your coachee *"That's not good enough. I think you can do better than that and I am here to help you stretch your potential in this area"*. If not, why not? Could you imagine yourself saying *"Here is your 360 feedback report? It shows that, in the eyes of others, you are a star. Given this feedback, I am wondering whether you could have a more ambitious vision for yourself and your career. I am wondering if you have a bigger contribution to make and what might be holding you back from doing this?"* If not, why not?

Does holding back from strong challenges of this type serve your coachee's development? Or are your reasons due to your own limited vision for the coachee, your fear of their potential and maybe your fear of your own potential to be a transformative coach?

Do you secretly 'laugh' at your coachees when they describe their own version of the 'Olympic gold medal'?

In order to learn more about putting challenge into practice it is worthwhile looking at what can be learnt from sports coaching. In sports coaching, challenge is a more accepted means of motivating and inspiring top performers to fulfil their potential. 121partners co-founder, Bill Barry, an Olympic medallist himself, has coached Alan Campbell from anonymity to becoming a world class sculler. This quote neatly summarises the start of their coaching relationship:-

"Alan Campbell's story is quite remarkable. Little more than a novice sculler when he first met his coach, Bill Barry, five years ago, he confidently declared that his ultimate

67

goal was to win Olympic gold. Some would have laughed but Barry recognised a spark of something exceptional in Campbell and decided to take him at his word." (Boardroom Magazine, September/October 2008).

In August 2009, Alan Campbell won the silver medal at the rowing world championships in Poland, breaking the current world record in the process.

Bill and Alan have a unique partnership as coach and athlete and their story is an inspiring example of the total belief of a coach in an athlete's potential and how such a belief can act as an empowering challenge to pursue the dream goal. Do you secretly 'laugh' at your coachees when they describe their own version of the 'Olympic gold medal' or do you take them at their word and begin the journey in partnership and with conviction?

Without challenge people cannot reach their higher selves. Only if we are willing to walk over the edge can we become winners.

In their work together, what enables Bill to challenge Alan effectively is partly that Alan respects Bill's own achievements and knows that Bill is not asking him to do something that he has not done himself (or would be prepared to do himself given a second chance!). He is credible. Also, Alan has worked with Bill over many years and in this time has learnt to trust Bill's intentions. In the context of such a well established relationship, Bill can 'push' Alan harder than would be the case if they had just met or if Bill had sent mixed messages about whether he really had Alan's best interests at heart.

Alan describes this impact of Bill's challenges as like *"having an extra person in the boat with me when I am racing"* - it motivates him alongside his own self-motivation and allows him to deal with the 'highs and lows' of winning and losing in this most competitive of sports. If Bill's challenges were ever to go too far then Alan is a strong enough individual to 'push back' and to be aware of his own limits. He has the confidence to keep the relationship a healthy partnership rather than lose ownership of his own destiny. Without challenge people cannot reach their higher selves. Only if we are willing to walk over the edge can we become winners.

Challenge Exercise

- Think of the example of the coaching partnership between Bill Barry and Alan Campbell.

- Ask yourself the question – Who fulfils this role in my life? Who challenges me? Who believes in me unconditionally and has a vision of my potential which inspires me?

- Once you have identified this person, ask yourself what it is about the relationship you have with this person that enables them to challenge you? Why is it that they can 'get away' with saying certain things to you that, coming from others, you would not accept or you would push away?

- When this person challenges you, how do they do it effectively? What tips and tricks could you learn from them that might help you as a coach challenge your coachees more effectively? What is the impact of their challenges on you?

- Can you discern the difference between this positive impact and the negative impact that other forms of 'challenge' could have on you?

- Finally, what happens when this person goes too far in challenging you? Is this possible? How do you deal with that and how might this relate to your coaching relationships?

Case Study - Challenge

An international business has started a leadership development programme for its European directors. This nine month programme is to strengthen leadership capability and develop an integrated team which is essential to bring about a swift recovery following the economic downturn. One of the key elements of the programme is a 360 degree assessment based on the company's leadership competencies. This will provide individual focus for the development programme. Participants are supported by six coaching sessions provided by an external coach.

Emma is one of the participants and has been with the business for five years, performing well, and promoted 18 months ago.

The coach matching process and the initial chemistry/contracting meeting with Emma has taken place and you are her chosen coach. At the second session you discussed the 360 feedback which was consistently good. On a scale of zero (low) to five (high), Emma scored fours and fives, and her self-assessment is in line with that of others. This confirmed that all is well and her performance is recognised. In terms of future development, however, the 360 does not help provide focus. As a result, you finish the coaching session feeling that there is no clear development plan for Emma and that the coaching may slip into nice conversations without an objective or clear outcome. You both agree to tackle this in the next session.

The FACTS Response

The lack of clear focus for the coaching is of concern. The company has taken a risk investing in a large programme in the current economic climate and needs to see a return on investment with the coaching having an 'edge' and 'bite'.

Often development plans from 360's focus on plugging gaps where the participant has scored low. Clearly addressing these gaps are an important part of the 360 approach. However the coach must not miss the opportunity to explore strengths, and develop awareness of hidden strengths. As Emma's self-assessment is consistent with feedback from others, it seems that she is aware of her strengths (if she had scored lower than the other assessors, this may indicate hidden strengths).

In this example, there is still much more the coach can do to stretch Emma. Another anecdote from sport is helpful to explore this assertion: In the 2008 Beijing Olympics athletics, Usain Bolt won two gold medals and at the same time set two new world records. In August 2009, during the World Athletic Championships, Usain won three gold medals and again set two new records. Commentators were asking 'how good could he be?', and we wonder what Usain's coach said to him after Beijing. Usain Bolt could have decided not to try any more as he had achieved a gold medal and a world record. However, he chose to aim higher and achieve more. It seems that no matter how good people are, they have the capability to be even better. World record holders can shave off an extra hundredth of a second. In a similar way Emma could be even better - if she wants to.

So returning to Emma, the FACTS coach could challenge Emma to identify how great she could be. The coach might say *"Let's go through your*

360 and focus on the areas where you are really strong – looking at the wider needs of your organisation what could you do to turn this strength into something really exceptional"?

Emma may need pushing to visualise and achieve her 'world record', her 'personal best', and her 'gold medal'. She may be challenged to identify this in concrete tangible terms so the goal becomes real rather than just an aspiration. Emma is a high achiever and can be stretched with statements like *"I believe you are capable of more…what more can you do?"* and not accepting Emma's first response, demanding that Emma thinks harder. The challenge could be significant by the coach saying *"that is not good enough; I think you are selling yourself short; aim higher!"*. Stories like Usain Bolt's can be used, along with powerful silence and simple questions asked like *"what else?"* to move Emma towards a concrete, motivational and stretching objective.

Key Learning Points

- Unlike feedback and accountability, effective challenge is focussed on future goals

- Executive coaching can learn a lot from observing how challenge is used effectively in sports coaching to motivate top performers

- Effective challenge needs to be supported by the total belief of the coach in the coachee

- A lack of challenge in coaching can allow complacency to creep into the relationship

- Challenge by the coach combined with the self motivation of the coachee can deliver exceptional results.

Tension

Tension Theory

The "T" in the FACTS approach is possibly the hardest skill for the coach to master and yet is critical to gaining the optimum performance outcome from coaching. The link between performance and tension is represented in Figure 5.

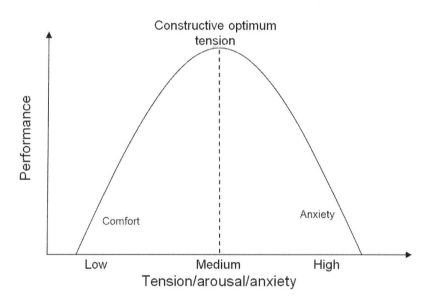

Figure 5

Tension can be described as arousal or anxiety. As arousal increases, performance increases to an optimum level and then tails off. The relationship between arousal and performance (the Yerkes-Dodson law), was identified by two psychologists in 1908 (Yerkes & Dodson, 1908), and subsequent research by other psychologists has confirmed this correlation (Anderson, Revelle, & Lynch, 1989).

Their law dictates that performance increases with physiological or mental arousal up to an optimal level. When levels of mental arousal pass this optimal point performance decreases. This performance-tension curve relates to mental and physical tasks. It can be said that there are two halves to the performance-tension curve. The left-hand upward part of the inverted U is the energising effect of arousal, while the right-hand downward part is caused by negative effects of over-arousal such as stress.

Sometimes there is a negative interpretation of the word tension. Tension has become associated with stress and something that should be avoided. However, tension can also be thought of as potential energy. Imagine a rubber band that is stretched, as the tension of the band increases it holds more energy. Think about a child flicking a rubber band by holding one end of the band over the thumb of his left hand and stretching the other end with the thumb and forefinger of his right hand. The more the child stretches the band then the more tension there is and so, when the child releases the grip, the band will fly through the air. The more stretch, the more energy and so the band will travel further. If there is not enough energy, the band will flop to the floor. However if the child stretches and stretches the band and does not release it, eventually the tension becomes too great and the band snaps.

Tension has become associated with stress and something that should be avoided.

So there is an optimum level of tension, too little will not maximise performance and too much will lead to destruction. In coaching it could be said that the left hand end of the horizontal axis is 'comfort', the right hand end is 'anxiety'. Neither maximise performance but in the middle there is creative space. There are two implications for coaching. First, is there enough tension for the coach to perform at his or her optimal level? Second, is there enough tension for the coachee to perform at their optimal level?

Tension in Practice

Feedback, Accountability and Challenge depend heavily on the verbal communication skills of the coach, whereas Tension relies much more on the non-verbal skills of managing this potential energy in the conversation. Through continued personal development and self-awareness, the coach can become aware of optimal levels of tension and arousal. On a very simple level this can be done by considering the emotional state of the coach as the coach entered the session. Did they feel comfortable and easy, or was the coach nervous and anxious? Linked with this, after the session the coach can assess his/her effectiveness during the session and so correlate their own 'performance versus tension model'.

> *The big difference between counselling and coaching is not what the practitioners do; it's who they are working with.*

When considering the optimal level of tension for the coachee, the coach can consider the conditions that are created in the coaching session and if this produces the optimal level of tension or not. This awareness is

77

very important since many coaches believe tension should be low and sessions should be as relaxed as possible.

One explanation for this is the link coaching has with the 'sister' profession of counselling. The big difference between counselling and coaching is not what the practitioners do; it's who they are working with.

Typically people who go and see counsellors are often saying: *"I'm not functioning properly and I want to be fixed and feel better."* The person seeing a counsellor is likely to have high levels of tension or anxiety and may already be in the sub-optimal level area of performance. If this is the case, the counsellor will consciously create the conditions to reduce tension and anxiety and hold a very relaxed session to bring the coachee to the optimal level of arousal. As a result, the amount of tension that a person in this state can take is much lower than your average senior executive in a major company who is usually functioning well and not in need of therapeutic input. Many people in business actually thrive on tension. So as coaches we're talking about highly effective people who are not declared dysfunctional and can often take much more tension than coaches believe they can.

> *The coachee may actually be capable of maximising performance and working at higher levels of tension than suits the coach.*

In training, coaches are often taught about the power of silence and encouraged to hold the silence and not to rescue people from silence. Silence is a way of increasing the tension. Silence encourages the coachee to think deeper, to reflect more, and to be more creative. This tension can be a hugely constructive energy if it is used and managed in an appropriate way. However, holding the tension and not feeling responsible for defusing the tension and making it more comfortable is something that a lot of coaches struggle with.

So how does a coach know the right level of tension? Each coachee will have a natural starting point of arousal and tension, which will indicate the position of the optimal level of tension. Each activity and task will produce different levels of tension which will vary for each person. So the coach is back in the 'learning laboratory', experimenting with interventions and observing cause and effect. The coach can gauge and test for the optimal level of arousal by creating tension and evaluating the reaction. Each intervention is consciously designed by the coach to identify the optimal level of tension. If the session feels too easy and relaxed, the coach can intervene and create more tension, to test the coachee more and make him/her work harder.

The key to this is the orientation and skill of the coach. The coach believes whole heartedly in the coachee's greatness, so the tension that the coach creates will be for a positive reason. *"As a coach, I believe you can achieve greatness and can do more, and so I will push you…"* In this context, the tension created by coaching is positive. The skill of the coach is to spot when the coachee's performance decreases, and so not go beyond the optimal level of tension. The coachee may actually be capable of maximising performance and working at higher levels of tension than suits the coach.

For example, imagine a coaching session in which the coachee role played being the chief executive because he had to make a decision about a new way of structuring the organisation. The coach put the coachee in the chief executive's position and said, *"Okay, if it was your business, what would you do?"* The coachee said, *"I don't know what I'd do,"* to which the coach's response was *"You've got to make a decision - you're the boss."* Following this intervention, the coach fell silent and allowed the tension in the session to rise as the coachee grappled with the ultimatum they had been given. Eventually, the coachee declared *"I've got it! It is not about the structure at all. No structure would resolve this problem - we just need to work better as a team and that's where I want to focus my energy."*

In this way, it can be seen that if coaches hold the view that tension is negative and destructive, and should be avoided at all cost, they might be 'selling their coachees short'.

Tension Exercise

- Reflect on coaching sessions or any other meetings in which you felt the tension build and consider the following:
    - What was happening at the time?
    - What are the themes and common features in your examples?
    - What did you do with the tension and how did you react?
- Discuss with your supervisor your thoughts and reflections on how you respond to tension and then how this impacts on your coaching.
- In coaching pairs discuss a controversial topic and take opposing views. For example Person A starts the discussion with the statement *"Gordon Brown is a great Prime Minister because...."* After which Person B responds with *"I disagree, because..."* Allow the disagreement to take place and continue for a few minutes then pause and review what happened, how you and the other person felt and responded, and how this has impacted on your relationship.

Case Study - Creating Tension

A Managing Director, Steve, has received negative feedback from his colleagues regarding the performance of his Sales & Marketing Director, Brian. Whilst Brian is delivering stunning results, he is considered to be a poor communicator. In particular, he is perceived to show disrespect for his seniors, avoiding opportunities to share information and appearing rude when in meetings and conference calls.

Steve believes that Brian is being naive about the politics of the organisation, risking his future progression despite his obvious potential. Brian's view is that the organisation is ridden with febrile politics and has no respect for the culture of senior management. His self confidence is such that he is prepared to leave the organisation and get a new role rather than 'play the game'.

Steve has engaged you as a coach with Brian's full support. In your initial three-way contracting discussion, Steve states that he expects Brian to shift the perceptions of key senior managers in one month via a 'blitz' of communication activity. He has even drafted the contents of this communication 'blitz' prior to the meeting and presents these to Brian as a 'fait accompli'. Brian does not react and appears very accepting of Steve's expectations.

However, at your first one to one coaching session, whilst discussing the goals and measures of success for the coaching programme, it becomes clear that Brian has not 'bought into' the goals Steve has presented. Where do you go from here if you are following the FACTS approach?

The FACTS Response

At this point, as the coach, you take a step back to gauge the tension that exists for Brian in this situation. Whilst, in theory, this is a situation in which many executives would feel great pressure, due to the negative feedback and the high expectations, you realise that Brian is not feeling this pressure and has a 'laid back' attitude.

In response to this, you decide to 'ramp up' the tension by stating to Brian *"It is clear to me that you are not committed to the goals that Steve has set for this coaching and yet you did not openly challenge these goals in our three way meeting. As your coach, I am unable to commit to this assignment because I do not believe we have the conditions to deliver a 'win/win' solution for you and your employer."* At this, Brian leans forward and appears to get more engaged. *"But your role is to support me in this process, to help me improve my communication skills"* he replies. *"Yes, that is true, but only if I believe that we have alignment between your goals and those of the sponsor of this coaching, namely Steve. Currently, I do not think you are being honest with Steve about your reaction to his expectations. I am not interested in being part of a 'covert operation' to pay 'lip service' to Steve's expectations and create an alternative agenda".*

The tension gauge has jumped to another level but is not yet 'red lining'. You realise that Brian can handle this level of tension and that it is provoking him to think and to engage. *"Well, how do you suggest we handle this, then?"* he barks, getting a little agitated. The agitation in his voice gives you a clue that you are at risk of losing the rapport to an extent that may be too damaging to the relationship. Remembering the balance between the 'building relationships' and 'driving for results' coaching skills, you now choose to hold the tension at its current level and throw Brian a follow up question – *"I am not sure. What do you think would be a 'win/win' outcome for both you and Steve in this situation?"*

Right now, the atmosphere in the coaching session is heavy with tension and frustration. Part of you wants to make things easier for both of you by offering a suggestion or backing off from your original position or by changing the subject and asking him where the toilets are!

After what seems like an eternity, Brian turns to look you in the eye and says *"I need to go back to Steve and let him know that his expectations for this coaching work are unrealistic. I need to re-negotiate the goals and measures of success with him and get to a place where both of us have a shared agenda."*

You sit back, let out all the tension in the system with an audible sigh of relief, and say *"Well done, Brian, well done. You have already started to improve your communication skills with senior management."*

Key Learning Points

- Tension is about creating an atmosphere in which the coachee achieves optimal performance

- Tension can be constructive or destructive depending upon the individual and the situation

- Because of its historical links to counselling, coaching has sometimes erred on the side of avoiding tension

- The coach must learn the optimum level of tension for themselves and the coachee to achieve optimum performance in the coaching session

- High achieving people can often operate at a higher level of tension than even the coach – so calibrate tension using their scale not yours!

Systems Thinking

Systems Thinking Theory

Finally, we reach the 'S' of FACTS which represents 'Systems Thinking'; a skill very different to any of those we have discussed in the model so far. 'Systems Thinking' is about the awareness of the 'bigger picture' and a willingness of the coach to help the coachee explore this.

When you are sat with a coachee, it can sometimes be tempting to think that they are an 'island' and that their actions are independent of what is happening in the rest of the organisation. This way of thinking can lead to a focus upon maximising their performance irrespective of the environment in which they are operating, optimising their behaviour without regard to the impact on their team or peers. Within the FACTS approach we place a much greater emphasis on considering the implications of actions and impacts on the wider organisation and beyond.

When the bank traders were at work in the 'boom' years, their goal was often to maximise their own personal bonuses irrespective of the wider consequences of their actions. There were many high profile cases of traders that took this approach to the limit and took risks that jeopardised the viability of the entire organisation. The warning signs were there many years before the 'credit crunch' that suggested that the actions of one individual could generate both 'desirable results' but also 'unintended consequences' in other parts of the banking system. There had already been well documented cases of rogue traders, like Nick Leeson, bringing banks to their knees through their isolated actions (Leeson, 1997).

85

As the habit of this behaviour spread in the early 21st century, it was ultimately the collation of all these 'unintended consequences' which led to a breakdown of trust in the whole banking system. In a sense no one person was responsible for this 'crunch' but, in another sense, all participants in the system were equally responsible. Whilst systems thinking is a discipline that has existed for many years and was brought into the mainstream of business thinking via books like 'The Learning Organisation' in the nineties (Senge, 2006), it seems that systems thinking is still regarded as an academic concept and not a principle by which people should live their lives.

Whenever we coach in a corporate context, we become an active part of that wider organisational system. It is one thing for us to be confidential, independent and detached but this does not mean that we can ignore the wider impacts of our work. In chaos theory, there is the famous example of how a butterfly flapping its wings in South America could be the cause of a tornado in Japan due to the complex inter-related global system that is our weather (Lorenz, 1995). How do you know when you are coaching that you might not also be such a 'butterfly' and the 'flapping of your coaching wings' may shift the energy in the system in such a way that significant impacts arise from your interventions?

Whenever we coach in a corporate context, we become an active part of that wider organisational system.

If you accept this principle of systems thinking and the idea that actions taken in one part of a system will introduce both 'desired results' and also 'unintended consequences' then, as a coach, it raises the question of how you fulfil your responsibility to the system as well as your responsibility to the individual and to yourself. It asks you to balance these interests and perspectives proactively rather than to blindly focus upon the individual in a style that may collude with an 'island mentality'.

One reaction to this dilemma is for coaches to slip into judgement around 'what the system wants' - to believe that they know the 'big answers' to the 'big questions' and to think that their role is to impose this worldview onto the coachee regardless of the coachee's own values and perspectives. An example would be a coach who is passionate about the environment and who allows this passion to show up in their coaching in a way that uses a subtle 'guilt-trip' to manipulate a coachee's outlook and actions.

> *One reaction to this dilemma is for coaches to slip into judgement around 'what the system wants'.*

Such an approach risks treading on a slippery slope that, at best, leads the coach into a mentoring role or, at worst, stigmatises them as evangelical change agents who will alienate as many coachees as they attract. Neither stance feels like it ought to be the future path of a mature coaching profession.

Faced with the options of doing nothing or stepping into judgement, the FACTS approach introduces a 'third way' – the practice of using powerful, systems thinking questions to raise the coachee's self awareness around the wider implications of their thinking and behaviour. Such questions are designed to broaden the coachee's sphere of responsibility. Whilst they are most definitely leading questions, they do not assume that the coach knows the 'right answer' but they do challenge the coachee to expand their thinking.

Figure 6, originally developed by Sir John Whitmore (Whitmore, 'Make a Difference Now' ICF keynote presentation, 2008), shows the intended impact of systems thinking questions. At the centre of a person's identity is themselves, the 'me' on which they have naturally learnt to focus through the course of 'day to day' life. People with this focus are viewed as 'looking after No.1' and, in western society, this is a well established cultural norm.

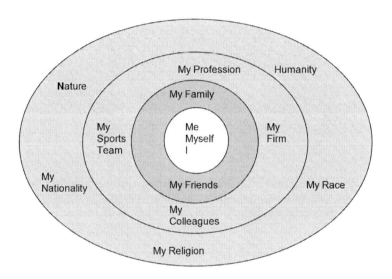

Figure 6

In the 'boom' years, you could say that we experimented with the extreme edges of the 'me, me, me' culture. Stepping outside 'Me' would lead people to think next about their families, their friends, their colleagues, etc. This is the first layer of 'Us'. Once 'Me' has taken care of No.1 then these would be the No.2, No.3 and No.4 that most people would then focus upon and care about. Stepping further out into the system, there are times when people will stretch their identity to include their race, their religion, their nationality. For example, in times of war or in competitive sport, these are identities which we call 'Us' and which we care about.

Ultimately, the systems thinking perspective subscribes to the belief that 'we are all one'. It suggests that, in the widest view, 'Us' represents nature, the universe, the planet, the entire human race. Whilst this is a level that most of us are not used to thinking at very often, there are now challenges facing us that are forcing us to do this, the most obvious one being the issue of climate change.

The systems thinking perspective, subscribes to the belief that 'we are all one'.

Systems Thinking in Practice

Bringing this back to coaching, the earlier diagram gives us a 'map' of possible perspectives from which to ask powerful, systems thinking questions. Such questions prompt the coachee to shift their level of thinking and look at the issue from a broader perspective. For example, you might be working with a coachee on the topic of their personal work/life balance. Questions that ask the coachee to consider the perspective of their family as well as their boss on such a topic are already bringing into play different stakeholders in the system.

You might be working with a coachee on a sensitive decision which involves a trade-off between profit and people. A simple question such as: *"If your decision were to be featured tomorrow on the front page of 'The Daily Telegraph' how would you feel about that?",* confronts the coachee to bring in the perspective of the general public, their friends, their family and so could shift their focus to many different levels of the system.

Finally, you may be working with a finance trader in the next 'boom' period who is focussed upon maximising their bonus payment by taking risks, the implications of which they do not fully understand. You might ask such a coachee *"If you were talking to your grandchildren in twenty year's time about this decision, how would you explain it to them?"* Such a question may 'jolt' the coachees thinking in a way that generates a healthy recognition of their wider role and identity beyond the workplace.

In the FACTS approach, we encourage coaches to create powerful questions that invite the coachee to explore the systems impact of their thinking from the following stakeholder perspectives:

- Customers

- Staff

- Shareholders

- Society

- Family

- Friends

You could view it as the coaching profession's contribution to the sustainability agenda!

Example coaching questions for each of these stakeholder perspectives might include:-

- *"How do you think your customers would react to this?"*

- *"In this situation, what could you do that would make your staff feel very proud to work for you and this company?"*

- *"If you owned this business then how would that change your thinking?"*

- *"If you were being profiled in the media as a great business leader in the 21st century, how would you like to be portrayed?"*

- *"Who in your family might be able to bring a valuable perspective to this challenge?"*

- *"Who is your best friend? What would their advice be to you right now?"*

This is not an exhaustive list and each coach will find their own versions of these questions 'in the moment' with their coachee. The purpose of the FACTS approach is to raise the coaching profession's own awareness of its role in the wider system and invite coaches to take responsibility for this without compromising the non-judgemental stance of the coaching philosophy. You could view it as the coaching profession's contribution to the sustainability agenda!

Systems Thinking Exercise

Work in trios with two coaching partners. Take turns to coach each other on a typical workplace topic with the third coach acting as observer. Whoever is coaching is encouraged to expcriment with asking creative, systems thinking questions relevant to the topic. The role of the observer is to identify these questions and to feedback the observed impact of the question on the coachee. The aim is for the coach to invite the coachee to explore the topic from at least three different stakeholder perspectives. After twenty minutes, debrief the exercise and then switch roles. In the de-brief consider the following questions:

- How did it feel to ask a systems thinking question? (coach)

- How did it feel to be asked a systems thinking question? (coachee)

- What was the observed impact on the coachee and on the course of the coaching session? (observer)

- What might have happened if the systems thinking perspective had not been explored by the coach? (All)

- Could you imagine asking these questions in 'real life' with a senior executive and what might inhibit you? (All)

- What risks and opportunities do you see in taking a systems thinking approach in your coaching? (All)

Case Study - Systems Thinking

You have been approached by a major UK organisation to coach a newly appointed senior leader, Katherine. In the criteria for selecting you as her coach, Katherine stresses that she is particularly interested in your spiritual outlook and wishes you to bring this to the coaching engagement, alongside your business experience. The focus of the coaching programme is building confidence in the first 100 days of the new role. In the first session, it soon becomes clear that Katherine is surprised to have been promoted and has found herself in a very challenging political environment. She is even questioning whether the organisation made the right decision in promoting her since she feels like a 'fish out of water' in the new role. Confidence is ebbing away as Katherine haunts herself with the thought that she and the organisation have made a big mistake. Where do you go from here if you are following the FACTS approach?

The FACTS Response

When Katherine states that she feels like 'a fish out of water' this is communicating to you that she does not feel at home in the current system. Therefore, using the FACTS approach, it triggers your system thinking awareness and encourages you to explore the context further.

You ask Katherine *"What do you think is your purpose in this political system?"* and, quick as a flash, the response comes *"To change it!"* *"And when you were chosen for the role, what do you think your new boss was expecting of you?"* you follow up, seeking to gain a view from the line manager's perspective. *"To change the current way of doing things"*, she replies, reinforcing the reasons for her being in this role right now.

"So it seems that you and your boss agree that your role is to change this system and therefore I am not surprised that you feel like 'a fish out of water' right now" you reflect before continuing *"What is your highest vision for the reason you are a change agent in this system?"*. This question invites the coachee to expand their thinking several levels further 'out' from their immediate 'here and now' environment. *"I believe that people want a different style of leadership in the world right now."* Katherine replies *"I think they are sick of the old ways and are demanding that organisations like ours re-invent themselves to present a more human, caring, authentic face to the world."*

At this stage, Katherine is tapping into a deep, personal purpose and drawing strength and confidence from the vision she holds around leadership. She is sensing that she is not alone and that many others share this vision even though they might not be in her immediate political system.

"And do you feel like a fish out of water now?" you venture, *"No, not from that perspective. From that perspective, I feel part of an inspiring movement of people and I can understand why this role is exactly the right role for me to be doing right now"*, she replies.

"And what do you want your grandchildren to say of you when they speak of your time as a leader in business?" you ask.

"I want them to feel proud of me, to know that I was brave and that I had a vision and that I pursued it despite the obstacles and barriers along the way. I want them to think that I was part of the solution and not part of the problem."

The sense of a shift in Katherine's confidence is palpable at this point in the coaching session. Reconnecting with her wider purpose and vision has empowered her. As the coach, you can now work with this empowerment to generate action and commitment.

"Who else can support you in this role now that you have seen your higher purpose?" you ask.

"Well, I would never have thought of this before but I can see that spending time with Peter, my old boss, who now heads up the accounts function, would be very helpful. Peter shares my vision and is a change agent in his own way. I will arrange to have lunch with him and use this as an opportunity to compare notes on how we view the organisation right now".

"And how about your boss, what feels like the next step in that relationship?"

"I am 90% sure that my boss recruited me to be a change agent but it would help me to have the conversation directly with him to eliminate that final 10% of doubt in my mind. I have been avoiding this conversation for fear that I might have got the 'wrong end of the stick' but I can now see this is just leaving me in 'no man's land".

"Great!" you conclude *"your vision is inspiring and it sounds like you are in exactly the right place at exactly the right time".*

Key Learning Points

- Systems Thinking stretches the coachee to consider the widest possible implications of their actions

- Systems Thinking is particularly relevant when times are tough and the usual answers don't work any more

- The role of the coach is to raise awareness by asking Systems Thinking questions – not to evangelise on their views

- Systems Thinking will shift the perspective of the coachee and may lead to unexpected 'breakthroughs'

- The FACTS approach encourages optimising the outcome for the 'system' as a whole rather than any one individual stakeholder

Contracting and Supervision with FACTS

Contracting and FACTS

Much of the effectiveness of coaching is based on how the relationship starts. This is about contracting, i.e. establishing the physical, psychological and financial terms and conditions for the coaching relationship. A professional coach working with a coachee will also be in 'supervision'. So we will consider how supervision within the FACTS framework is similar or different to typical supervision. As Stephen Covey puts it - how do coaches 'sharpen the saw'? (Covey, 2004). First, let's take some time to look at traditional contracting and then focus on FACTS contracting.

'As Stephen Covey puts it - how do coaches 'sharpen the saw'?

Contracting has always been seen as an essential part of the coaching relationship. Both the ICF and the AC describe contracting in their core competencies (AC Core Competencies, 2005), (ICF Core Competencies, 1999). Contracting is also discussed in a number of coaching books and typically there are the following elements to contracting:

- Ethics and standards of conduct, appropriate behaviour

- Confidentiality

- Boundaries, understanding the distinction between coaching and therapeutic interventions such as psychotherapy and counselling and when to involve other professions

- Logistical arrangements, such as the location for meetings, length of each meeting, duration of the coaching assignment, fees, cancellation charges, etc.

- Involvement of third party stakeholders (sponsors of the coaching such as line managers or Human Resource professionals from an organisational context)

- Monitoring and Evaluation

- Ending the coaching relationship

The purpose of contracting is to set out at the beginning of the assignment the parameters of the coaching and so the coachee understands 'what the deal is' and what to expect. In this way, the foundation is set and coach, sponsor and coachee enter the relationship with 'eyes open' and with a clear and shared understanding.

At the height of the utilisation of coaching in the 'boom' times, contracting conversations were often short, covering confidentiality and ethics only.

Beyond this the contract boundaries are often undefined and unclear. At the height of the utilisation of coaching in the 'boom' times, contracting conversations were often short, covering confidentiality and ethics only. Sometimes the coachee could choose to use the coach or not during a leadership development programme, and the topics discussed could be wide ranging based on the agenda of the coachee. Contracting of this type is like holistic coaching i.e. there is one person being coached who has a life inside work which obviously overlaps with their life outside work,

98

so coach the whole person and there will be an impact within the business. So working on the coachee's agenda was core for many coaches and this worked within the loose contracting framework.

Amongst coaches there is often a debate about who the real client is. Is it the coachee, the person in front of them being coached, or is it the company sponsoring and paying for the coaching? Some coaches say that their prime responsibility is to the coachee which leads to sessions being too person focussed and unrelated to the organisation which is sponsoring the coaching. The confidentiality agreed in the contract often prevents the sponsoring organisation knowing anything more except that the coaching session has taken place.

This broad contracting may have contributed to the negative perception by some business people that executive coaching was no different to life coaching with no relevance to the business and with no way of demonstrating a return on investment.

However, in the FACTS coaching approach, contracting goes further and deeper, detailing what the coachee can expect in terms of feedback, accountability, challenge, tension and systems thinking. This is very much about clarity of coaching presence and the coach 'showing up fully' at the start of the coaching assignment, being bold, stating *"this is what I do, this is how I do it, this is what you (the coachee) can expect from me, and this is what I expect of you (as a coachee). As a FACTS coach I'm going to bring something extra which I believe is an important component to convert the strong coach and coachee relationship into results".* In a FACTS contracting discussion, we would expect each element of the approach to be specifically contracted with both the coachee and the organisation sponsor. For example:

Feedback

The coach discusses with the coachee the importance of feedback and that the coach has a unique perspective to provide feedback to highlight hidden strengths or uncover 'blind spots'. The coach will provide feedback to develop the self-awareness of the coachee with the belief that awareness leads to action and so greater choices for the coachee. The coach will not ask for permission to provide feedback, and feedback will be frequent and on-going.

Accountability

How does the coachee wish the coach to hold them accountable for actions? This is an explicit discussion with the coachee along the lines of *"Before we start, I really want to have a discussion with you about accountability. If we work together you have to understand that I'm going to hold you accountable, that's the way I work. I will expect you to undertake actions that you agree to undertake. If you don't do an action how do you want me to handle it?"*

Challenge

> *"Before we start, I really want to have a discussion with you about accountability."*

What does effective challenge mean to the coach and the coachee? The coach and coachee have a clear conversation to agree how to challenge. For example if the coachee appears to be resisting or avoiding the challenge, it will cover how the coach will address this. However, the explicit agreement is that the coach will challenge the coachee, will expect 'stretch' and depth of thought and will expect the coachee to work harder as the relationship develops. This may be by simple statements such as *"I think you can do better than that, think again"*, or *"what else could you do?"*, or *"what more could you do?"* The coach will ask these questions, and not let the coachee 'off the hook'; the challenge is made by the coach in a confident and self-assured way, consistent with what has been agreed in the initial contracting discussion.

Tension

The contracting will determine what level of tension is optimum for the coachee to maximise performance. This may be an uncomfortable discussion because it is about the coachee and the coach moving outside the comfort zone. Development and personal growth comes from the stretch into the unknown, to take an extra step, to do something different, to do something more. The breaking of old habits and introduction of new habits that are reinforced by practice can be challenging. The coach needs to be able to hold the tension at these key moments. Again in the contracting discussion, the coachee needs to understand that this may not be an easy journey, there are likely to be difficult times when this feels uncomfortable. The coach can reassure the coachee that these feelings are normal, that the coach is experienced in handling tension constructively and that through this tension will emerge more profound end results.

Systems Thinking

What are the expectations of the wider system for the coaching assignment? As highlighted earlier, good practice is for the coach to take into account the views of other stakeholders to ensure the coaching assignment is strongly sponsored by the relevant organisational stakeholders. The FACTS approach requires that as many stakeholders as possible are considered throughout the coaching assignment and, particularly in the contracting conversation, the coach will ask *"which other stakeholders do we need to take account of, and how do we stay aligned to their needs? What are the measures of success from their perspectives? Is there sufficient alignment of goals and expectations across the system to commence this coaching with confidence and commitment?"*

Throughout the assignment the coach will be representing the interests of the other stakeholders and at times will ask *"what will your customers think about this; what is the long term impact of this on the sustainability of this company?"*

> With this more comprehensive contract in place, the coachee and their sponsor have a clear picture of what to expect from coaching.

This is not an evangelical crusade by the coach but is based on a logical analysis of the system and the interests of a wide body of stakeholders who have been identified 'up front' with the coachee.

Examples of stakeholders who would need to be involved in a FACTS contracting conversation would be line manager, HR manager, mentor, and other line managers upon whom the coachee's success is dependent. A three or four way contracting conversation may be necessary or a series of telephone call dialogues with different parties to assess the degree of alignment and commitment. The coach and coachee will then need to agree how each of these parties will be kept involved as the coaching proceeds, for example via a monthly update from the coachee or a mid-programme review.

With this more comprehensive contract in place, the coachee and their sponsor have a clear picture of what to expect from coaching, which goes beyond ethics and confidentiality and the frequency and duration of the coaching sessions. Similarly, the coach will have built the confidence and the permission to act in line with the FACTS approach without feeling that this will come as a surprise to the coachee. The coachee understands that an explicit part of 'the deal' is hard work and results. Why should the client of a coach expect less?

Once the coachee knows what to expect, he/she can decide to work with this coach, using the FACTS approach or not. The coach has the confidence and presence to say *"This is how I work; this is what you can expect because I know that this produces results. If you're comfortable that is great. If you're not comfortable, I'm not the right person to be working with you on this assignment."* Both parties can make a conscious choice to commit based on an honest sharing of expectations.

> "If you're not comfortable, I'm not the right person to be working with you on this assignment."

Throughout this process a coach using the FACTS approach will have the courage and the presence to walk away from a potential coaching assignment, rather than compromising on his/her approach.

Confidentiality and FACTS

Where does the principle of confidentiality fit in the FACTS approach? The FACTS approach expects results that will benefit the coachee and the sponsoring organisation. There could now be a conflict between maintaining confidentiality and keeping stakeholders informed and ensuring a return on the investment. How can a coach manage all of these demands?

The first thing to say is that confidentiality is an essential element of executive coaching, and this is a principle that must not be compromised. A relationship that is built on trust and that can move quickly to results can only be achieved with confidentiality. The confidential nature of the relationship with the external coach enables the coachee to be free from the normal constraints within an organisational environment. The coachee would be guarded on what was said and the areas of development if he or she felt that information was being fed back to the sponsor.

Confidentiality is a matter for explicit contracting upfront. Unless otherwise agreed in the contract, all communication should come from the coachee rather than the coach. Timely communication with stakeholders will enable all parties to trust the process and so lift the veil of secrecy that sometimes frustrates line managers. This approach proposes more structured feedback to the relevant audience.

For example, through the contracting process the coachee will agree to produce a monthly report on areas of development, progress and actions. The sponsors, typically the line manager, maybe the Human Resources Director and other key stakeholders will be given a copy of this report. There may be a mid programme review meeting with the coach, coachee, line manager and Human Resource Director to assess progress and review objectives. A final end-of-programme de-brief and planning session will complete the process with all stakeholders engaged.

Through this approach, communication is enhanced whilst confidentiality is maintained. There is an 'alignment of minds' for all the parties involved and a clear focus on performance results for the coachee and sponsoring organisation. An example template for a coaching agreement using the FACTS approach, which summarises all of the points covered regarding contracting, is included in Appendix 2.

Supervision and FACTS

There has been much written about the effectiveness of supervision in the continual professional development of a coach. A supervisor works with the coach to maintain and develop skills and professional standards. So what should a FACTS coach look for in a supervisor? This could be summarised as follows:

- Strong experience of working in corporations and organisations, so there is the empathy to relate to the business context

- Credible knowledge of coaching and supervision, which can be modelled and demonstrated

- The ability to mirror the FACTS approach, so that the supervisor is skilled (to the same level, and preferably to a higher level than the coach) in providing feedback, holding accountability, challenging, holding tension and considering the wider systems perspective.

Beyond these points, supervision using the FACTS approach serves the same purpose and has the same focus as supervision in any other coaching approach.

Case Study – FACTS Contracting

Fiona, the CEO of an IT services company, contacts you regarding one of her senior team. You have coached Fiona previously and have built considerable trust with her. She confides in you that a member of her team, Colin, has lost the support of his direct reports and the other Board members due to the perception that he is a 'bully'. However, Colin is delivering excellent 'bottom line' results and, for this reason, Fiona is reluctant to lose him but at a loss to know how to handle the situation.

Recently, Colin asked to see Fiona to discuss his future career development. He shared with Fiona that he had an expectation to be a successor for the CEO role and would have to consider his wider options if he was not regarded as a contender for this role in the future. Fiona created an excuse to bring the meeting to a close but promised to get back to Colin with answers to his questions. This was two months ago and Fiona is at a loss to know what to do. She asks if you will coach Colin because she knows how helpful coaching was for her in the past and thinks it would be helpful for him too.

As a FACTS coach, what do you do next?

The FACTS Response

"What a hornets' nest!" you think. The assignment is littered with boundary issues and ethical concerns. Five years ago, when you had just completed your original coaching qualifications, you would probably have 'run a mile' from this assignment, politely declining the request for help and then watching as Colin, Fiona and the organisation as whole continued to demonstrate dysfunctional behaviours that damage people and performance. Still, it's not your problem is it? It's their company after all and if they want to behave that way then it is up to them. You are not here to 'rescue' anyone and you could do without the hassle of getting involved in a 'no win' situation.

Still, there is part of you that nags away – *"Surely, there is a way to engage with this situation and help everyone move forward without compromising my ethics and principles as a coach. After all, if I, as a trusted and experienced coach, cannot offer help in this situation, who else can?"*

You sleep on it and then call Fiona in the morning:-

"Fiona, thanks for considering me for this work. It is clearly a complex, difficult problem that you want me to help with. If I am going to take on this assignment then there are some 'ground rules' that I need you to agree to, over and above our usual coaching agreement. Firstly, I would need you to be comfortable that I am working in the best interest of the 'system', i.e. the organisation as a whole, rather than serving either yours or Colin's needs in isolation. I would need both of you to agree to the definition of a 'win/win' outcome for the organisation and for that outcome to be discussed openly, documented and circulated to all parties that might have an interest and influence in this situation.

Secondly, Colin is clearly going to need some honest feedback if he is to understand the reality of the situation in which he is operating. I would need you to provide that feedback first hand to Colin before commencing any coaching and I would then want to follow up that conversation with a 360 feedback tool to be used prior to the first coaching session. Only if Colin is willing to take on board the feedback, and sees a reason to do something about it, do I think that this coaching could be successful.

Thirdly, I am sure that there will be occasions during this coaching when we encounter tense, sensitive issues. In these moments, I need you to be aware that I will not shy away from challenging either you or Colin if I sense that such an approach would release potential in the situation, even if it feels extremely awkward in the moment. Likewise, I will be holding both you and Colin accountable for, not only any actions either party commits to, but also for alignment between your words, actions, feelings, beliefs and values.

Finally, this 'tough love' approach may generate all sorts of tension and discomfort for you and Colin as the coaching proceeds. Whilst I hope you would trust the intention behind this approach, I realise that all parties, including myself, need to be able to disengage from the process at any point if it is not working true to these 'ground rules'."

There is a silence at the end of the phone and then Fiona comments:-

"Phew! That's quite a shopping list. And there was me thinking that I was offering you a valuable piece of work in a market that is very tough right now. I thought you might have been grateful for that, but it seems this could end up being more hassle than it is worth. Of the things that you have said, I suppose I could be comfortable with trying to find an organisational 'win/win' and also with providing feedback to Colin beforehand and the use of the 360 feedback tool. I know that challenge is an important part of your coaching. Neither Colin nor I are 'shrinking violets' so I don't see that as a problem. In fact I agree that it will be very necessary."

"However, this last point about you being able to disengage at any point in the coaching process if you think the 'ground rules' are not being met - I am not comfortable with that at all. As far as I am concerned, I am the customer and I am paying you to deliver a service and, really, if you start this, then I would insist that you follow it through to completion."

"Well, that's a shame, Fiona, a real shame. I do want to help and I do appreciate you offering me this work but I have to stay true to my ethics and integrity as a professional coach. I really can't take on this assignment on those terms and, reluctantly, I am going to have to say 'No' this time and hope that you and Colin find another way to move forward constructively".

"I'm disappointed too. You've let me down. Let's leave it at that".

…and with that, Fiona hangs up.

No one said that life would be easy as a FACTS coach!

Summary and Conclusions

This book is 121partners response to the need for the coaching profession to evolve and adapt to an ever moving, less stable world and business environment. There is no doubt that the collapse of a number of major financial institutions in late 2008 has led inevitably to a re-examination by organisations of their priorities and needs for coaching and leadership development. We have explored how this has caused the focus of coaching to shift emphasis from building relationships and retaining talent towards achieving high performance and delivering results and how coaches need to expand their 'edgy' skills by being prepared more often, and more skilfully, to enter the ZOUD. In an environment where the 'business agenda' takes precedence over the 'personal agenda' the challenge for the practising coach is 'how can session two have the same impact as session four or five of a typical coaching programme?'.

Figure 7 shows that the goal of a FACTS coach is to have developed the presence by session two, to engage with the coachee on 'the heart of the matter' rather than dancing around the topic until both parties have no choice but to address it. As a result the impact of session two can be the same as the impact of session four or five of a traditional coaching approach. Through the strong foundation of relationship skills, the FACTS approach enables the coach to accelerate the process of delivering results.

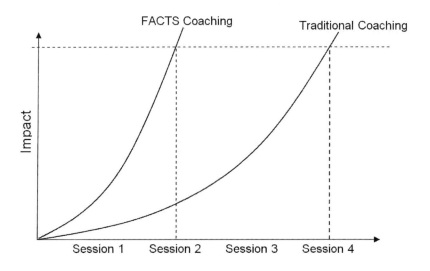

Figure 7

We see FACTS coaching as an approach that will be used to deliver this change of emphasis. And to do this effectively requires a much greater skill and focus on the five core components of FACTS: Giving effective and timely Feedback; holding the coachee Accountable for their action/non action; Challenging the coachee to achieve ever higher results; engaging with the coachee at a level of Tension that sustains optimum performance; and lastly taking a Systems Thinking approach that opens up the coachee's perspective to consider the widest possible implications of their decisions.

In considering effective feedback we promote the 4 stage model of observation, input, impact and action as a mechanism to allow the coach to provide feedback to the coachee in a non-aggressive and constructive way. We hold the coachee accountable for their actions through 'positive confrontation and reflection' on where/when the coachee is not meeting theirs and their organisation's own stated standards. In challenging, we use the sports analogy of high performance athletes competing and evermore breaking their own records as a testament to the ability of the 'human being' to achieve 'breakthrough results'. Our approach to 'managing tension' is built on well understood psychological models that allow this potential energy to be used constructively in facing difficult issues. Our multi layered 'systems thinking' model is remarkable in its simplicity, yet surprisingly underused in the 'boom' times of the 20th and early 21st century when the 'me, me, me' approach prevailed.

We do not limit our application of this approach to our coaching presence. We turn the light on ourselves and in our engagements we ask *"Give us Feedback on how we are helping you to deliver your results"*. We stand up and with a clear conscience say that *"we are prepared to be held Accountable for our part in your development"*. We 'Challenge' ourselves to 'improve' and commit to seeking out the people who will challenge us further. In supervision, we are prepared to take the 'Tension' and accept the 'Feedback' that supports our development. Furthermore

'It is not the strongest of the species that survives or the most intelligent that survives. It is the one that is most adaptable to change' - Darwin

we believe that our 'Systems Thinking' approach does not contradict the 'person centred' approach, but expands out from the individual to the wider circles of influence around them - and this has been a motivating force in writing this book. Lastly in terms of contracting we believe in looking at both the individual and organisational needs and are prepared to 'walk away' if the contract is at odds with the stated aims of the client.

So where were all the coaches when the banks went down and what are they all doing now? It is the nature of evolution that major cataclysmic events precipitate the need for change and result in marked evolutionary step changes. Even when the business environment improves we believe the challenging times we have discussed are here to stay. It will take a generation to work though the consequences of the excesses of the 'boom' years. Just looking at the level of public debt of the western world reminds us of the scale of these issues. So the coaching profession cannot afford to be complacent and assume that 'business as usual' will just pick up again. Coaching is no different to any other profession during a recession; as Darwin said 'It is not the strongest of the species that survives, nor the most intelligent that survives. It is the one that is most adaptable to change' (Darwin, 1998).There may be some coaches and development professionals who read this book and recognise an approach they have already been taking. There will be some who see the need for change and will sharpen their skills, becoming even better coaches. Inevitably, some will fall by the wayside. Whatever happens, the coaching profession will be stronger and fitter as a result. At 121partners, we hope the FACTS approach is a worthwhile contribution to the ongoing dialogue and look forward to playing our full part as the profession evolves and matures.

Appendix 1   Feedback Model

Stage 1: Observed

This is about what is observed by the coach and is specific and factual, with a description of what happened. There are no value statements; it is about the 'act not the actor' and so not directly about the person. There's nothing good or bad, there is no judgement, it is just about what has happened and we avoid the 'you are…' statements.

What it is:	What it is not
"I would like to give you some feedback. You talked about your assertiveness when with your boss, I've mentioned this three times today and each time you have then changed the subject and talked about something else"	*"Let me tell you something, we've had a couple of meetings now, and you just don't seem to be getting to grips with this"*
"You identified the objective of improving your impact and influence, I've noticed that every time you talk you look down at your note book, and then there is no eye contact."	*"You are avoiding eye contact with me"*
"At our last two sessions you committed to meeting with your boss to discuss your role, but again you say you have not had time to do this."	*"You don't seem very motivated to meet up with your boss"*

Stage 2: Impact

This stage relates to the impact of what happened, and the assumptions the coach (or others) made as a result. Whenever an action takes place, we try to understand and explain by rationalising. We form mental hypotheses to help understand and interpret what another person has said or done. We start forming a judgement as we then try and figure out why and what has happened. So it is a useful perspective for the coach to share his/her assumptions and feelings based on what the coachee has said. This will help the coachee gauge the impact of their words and actions. The coach can play back 'this is what I've seen, this is my interpretation'.

What it is:	What it is not
"Based on this, my assumption is that you are avoiding the matter, maybe this is too difficult to talk about?"	*"I guess you're not committed to the coaching process"*
"When you do this I can't hear you very well, the energy level seems to drop and I feel that you may not be confident about what you are saying, and what you are saying loses impact"	*"You are very quiet today"*
"Based on this I could assume it is not important to you anymore?"	*"you are not putting enough importance on this"*

Some coaches may say they do not talk about the impact on them as this has nothing to do with the coachee and what he/she is trying to achieve. However, if the thoughts and feelings of the coach are examples of how other people (boss, peers, team members, etc.) may also interpret the actions of the coachee, then sharing this information is a valuable insight. The coachee may not have considered how other people see them and the interpretations that other people make to explain their actions and words.

Stage 3: Invite input

The next stage after playing back the impact of the behaviour is to find out what the coachee thinks about your comments and interpretation. The coach may prompt the coachee by providing his/her interpretation and then asking open questions such as 'how do you see this?' or 'what's your take on this'?

The coach may prompt the coachee by providing his/her interpretation and asking "what's your take on this?"

What it is:	What it is not
"How do you see it?"	*"Do you agree?"*
"What do you think about my assumption?"	*"Assuming I am correct…"*
"How do you think other people might interpret this?"	*"Has this happened before with other people?"*

Stage 4: Action

In the last stage we discuss 'what should be done'? This action is future focussed and constructive where 'something can be done'. A frustrating aspect of poor feedback is when nothing specific can be done. For example: *"when you are next with David be more dynamic"*. What does this actually mean? *"...be more dynamic"* has a different meaning for everyone and if the person cannot take action, then the feedback is of little value. It also occurs when feedback is given too late. For example *"I observe you weren't assertive enough! You should have..."* Feedback is only valuable if the coachee can do something about it, such as change their tone of voice, change the words used, consider another perspective. This is all future focussed, it is looking forward to how things could be different and is constructive feedback. The person can take it and build on it and do something about it. This links back to the intention of the coach as unconditional positive regard, coming from the perspective of a mutually respectful relationship.

What does this actually mean? "...be more dynamic" has a different meaning for everyone and if the person cannot take action, then the feedback is of little value.

What it is:	What it is not
"How can we make this easier to talk about, what is the first small thing you could do?"	*"you need to do more and make a greater effort"*
"Let's try an exercise, talk to me for five minutes about your most recent holiday and maintain eye contact as you speak"	*"you need to make more eye contact when you talk"*
"Can I suggest we role play the situation?"	*"you need to try harder"*

Appendix 2 FACTS Coaching Agreement

Here is an example coaching contract agreement that outlines in practice the FACTS based contracting process.

Coachee Name: Anne Example

This agreement, between coach, Ian Day, of 121partners Limited and the above coachee, will begin on 2nd January, 2010. The scope of the executive coaching package will comprise the preparation, delivery and follow up of 5 two hour coaching sessions over a period of six months. It will include 'ad hoc' telephone and e-mail support between each session as required. At the end of this period a formal review will be carried out to measure success and agree next steps.

The stakeholders to be consulted when identifying objectives, reviewing progress and to be kept informed on results are:

- Jane Jones, Director of Services

- David Smith, Human Resources Director

- Nigel Hughes, Managing Director, Subsidiary Business Unit

The business and personal goals which will be the focus of the coaching partnership will be:

- To present confidently in Board meetings and consistently deliver presentations that are informative and interesting

- To confidently work with other people to achieve objectives, either on a 1 : 1 or group basis

- To be able to effectively prepare for meetings and organise projects

The success of this coaching partnership will be measured by:

- Increased acceptance of proposals at Board meetings; consistently positive feedback following presentation; feeling of confidence when delivering presentation (personal assessment).

- Greater ability to influence and work effectively through other people; actively engage with other people; communicate and involve other stakeholders; feeling of support from others (personal assessment).

- Ability to identify and implement effective action plans to achieve objectives; meetings are successful and well organised; positive feedback from participants

All information provided to the coach by the coachee will be kept strictly confidential. The coachee will produce a short monthly report which will go to the stakeholders identified above and will cover areas of development, progress and action plans.

During the coaching sessions the coach will provide the coachee with feedback to help develop self-awareness. The coachee agrees to undertake actions following the coaching session and the coach will hold the coachee accountable for undertaking these agreed actions.

The coaching sessions will be intentionally challenging to facilitate the achievement of objectives and support sustained development for the coachee. This challenge may produce tension designed to optimise performance (this is not intended to be stressful which will lead to sub-optimal performance). The coachee agrees to provide feedback to the coach so that the level of feedback, accountability, challenge and tension is at an appropriate and constructive level.

The coach abides to the ethical and professional standards identified by the [ICF, AC].

If either party believes this coaching partnership is not working as desired, they will communicate this to the other and take action to rectify this. Any advice or suggestions given are based on helping the coachee to make his/her own decisions and should not be taken as authoritative.

The coachee and the coach agree to provide one another with a minimum of three working days' notice in the event it is necessary to reschedule a session. Sessions start from the scheduled time and any time lost due to lateness on the part of the coachee will mean that the time may be forfeited. Beyond 15 minutes the entire session may be forfeited. Equally, should the coach be late or unable to deliver the session at short notice then the session will be rescheduled and an additional free half hour coaching session offered as compensation.

Signed

Coach.............................. Date........

Coachee............................ Date........

Sponsor............................ Date.......

Bibliography

Association for Coaching Core Competencies (2005). http://www.associationforcoaching.com/about/ACCFrame.pdf .

Anderson, K. J., Revelle, W., & Lynch, M. J. (1989). Caffeine, impulsivity, and memory scanning: A comparison of two explanations for the Yerkes-Dodson Effect. Motivation and Emotion , 13, 1-20.

Axelrod, E. L., Handfield-Jones, H., & Welsh, T. A. (May 2001). The War for Talent – part two. McKinsey Quarterly .

Boardroom Magazine. (September/October 2008). Going for Gold. Boardroom Magazine . http://www.121partners.com/downloads/article_boardroom_1008.pdf

Bowman, C. (1995). Strategy workshops and top-team commitment to strategic change. Journal of Managerial Psychology, vol 10 , issue 8, pages 2 - 12.

Covey, S. R. (2004). The seven habits of highly effective people. ISBN: 1416502491

Darwin, C. (1998). The Origin of Species. Wordsworth Classics of World Literature. ISBN: 1853267805

ICF Core Competencies (1999). http://www.coachfederation.org/research-education/icf-credentials/core-competencies.

Leeson, N. (1997). Rogue Trader. ISBN-13: 978-0751517088

Lorenz, E. (1995). The Essence of Chaos. ISBN-13: 978-1857284546

Logan, G. (2008).
http://www.personneltoday.com/articles/2008/01/14/48969/war-for-talent-is-over-as-finance-sector-vacancies-slump-by.html .

Rogers, C. (2004). On Becoming a Person. ISBN-13: 978-1845290573

Senge, P. (2006). The Fifth Discipline. ISBN-13: 978-1905211203

Simkin & Yontef. (1993). An Introduction to Gestalt Therapy.
http://www.behavior.net/gestalt.html

Whitmore, Sir. J. (2008). 'Make a Difference Now' keynote presentation.
UK ICF Conference Proceedings.

Whitmore, Sir. J. (2002). Coaching for Performance. ISBN-13: 978-1857883039

Yerkes, R. M. & Dodson, J. D. (1908). The relation of strength of stimulus to rapidity of habit-formation. Journal of Comparative Neurology and Psychology , 18, 459-482.

About The Authors

John Blakey

Now a coach to international business leaders, John has held board level roles in a number of organisations, most recently as international managing director of leading IT services organisation, Logica. He was the first director of coaching of a FTSE250 company and his pioneering work in the field of executive coaching is widely featured in conferences and articles. He was a member of the UK International Coach Federation Board from 2007-2009.

Ian Day

With over 20 years experience in senior HR roles and having most recently been head of talent management for an international FTSE100 company, Ian has been a qualified executive coach for eight years and leadership development consultant for four years. Ian is a chartered member of the Institute of Personnel and Development and an active member of the Association for Coaching.

121partners

121partners is a leadership development and coaching consultancy that works with senior directors and their teams in business and the public sector.

With the goal of improving organisational performance, 121partners specialises in business performance and development programmes for leaders and their teams. Clients are FTSE250 companies and dynamic public sector organisations.

The consultancy's coaches work with board-level teams to define shared goals and development plans that align with organisational strategy and business priorities. Over a period of 8-10 months, the 121partner coaches help the team identify and exploit their strengths, overcome weaknesses and achieve results through a mixture of individual coaching, team workshops and psychometric profiling.

All the121partners team combine senior-level business experience with formal coaching qualifications, with one of the team working as a personal and sports coach with the Olympic rowing squad in preparation for the London 2012 Games.

If you have enjoyed reading this book, please take a moment to add a review at

www.amazon.co.uk.

If you are interested in our one day master class

'Where were all the coaches when the banks went down?'

featuring the FACTS coaching approach, please contact us via

info@121partners.com

For more details on 121partners, please refer to our web site at

www.121partners.com